ONLINE
MARKETING
HANDBOOK

the small business ONLINE MARKETING HANDBOOK

Converting Online Conversations to Offline Sales

Annie Tsai

WILEY

Library of Congress Cataloging-in-Publication Data:

Tsai, Annie, 1979–
   The small business online marketing handbook : converting online conversations to offline sales /
Annie Tsai.
      pages cm
   Includes index.
   ISBN 978-1-118-61538-6 (hardback); ISBN 978-1-118-77015-3 (ebk); ISBN 978-1-118-77013-9
(ebk) 1. Small business marketing. 2. Internet marketing. I. Title.
   HF5415.13.T747 2013
   658.8′72—dc23

                                                                                                2013020039

Printed in the United States of America
10 9 8 7 6 5 4 3 2 1

Contents

Introduction

The formula for success as a small business doesn't seem to have changed much since the beginning of time: bring a great product or service to the neighborhood (or village), and deliver exceptional service. Not too complicated, right? So if the formula is so straightforward, why are some small businesses failing while others are wildly successful?

Most of us are well aware that technology developments over the past 10 years have changed the way all businesses, no matter their size, market to and interact with their customers. People rarely make a purchase nowadays without securing prior validation from a source they trust, be it consumer rating websites, online testimonials, or simply a conversation with a friend or acquaintance. Consumers have found their voice on the web and are regularly having public discussions about exactly what they like and dislike. Given that my company Demandforce alone has helped its customers generate and syndicate millions of customer reviews for the web over the past several years, it's hard to ignore how powerful the consumer voice is.

This shift toward empowering the consumer voice has dramatically redefined the relationship between the browser, buyer, and seller over time, to the point that it's simply no longer an option to ignore the consumer voice. Businesses that embrace and leverage this shift quickly leap ahead of those that don't. The latter group—those companies that attempt to control the conversation and are therefore unable to evolve how they market themselves and deliver service in the new world—is destined to fail.

There are additional factors that successful small businesses focus on—things they want to do better than everyone else. First, they not only deliver exceptional service, but they also *build relationships* with their customers to generate a strong referral business. Then, they leverage those relationships online, making every recommendation a powerful referral engine for their business.

THE SOCIAL CONVERSATION IS STANDARD TO YOUR SUCCESS EQUATION

Whether you like it or not, people are talking to each other about their purchase experiences, both online *and* off. Small business owners still don't have a strong sense of what's happening in the offline world; for example, does the old adage that there are "five bad reviews for every positive good review" still hold weight? In 2012, consumers reported that offline word of mouth still accounted for 62 percent of the conversations around deal sharing.[1] But it's challenging for small businesses to measure how effective offline marketing, word of mouth, and referral programs are for them.

Alternately, online businesses have access to a wealth of hard data on a variety of factors, including how consumers are browsing the Internet and what they're doing with their time. If businesses know what they're looking for, they can get a much clearer picture of which aspects of their programs are effective, and which they should tweak a bit or even drop completely. Most important, the profusion of sharing taking place on the web gives everyone a good idea of whom consumers are engaging with, and what they're talking about.

The real challenge small businesses face in terms of influencing—or even *joining*—the online social conversation is that there is simply too much information out there. It's difficult to know where to start, where to focus, and where to invest the marketing dollars and time you have. For example, if you account for one in every seven minutes that people spend online globally, you'll find that Facebook seems to dominate the social conversation. Therefore, the obvious choice seems to be to sign up for Facebook ads. However, the context surrounding the kind of social conversation you have on Facebook depends on the type of business you're running, and who your customers are. It's important to have the right kind of conversation and invest in the right social channels. Otherwise, you could very well have no impact—or worse, a detrimental effect on your business.

You may already be aware of these as critical factors to success in today's online social economy. But let's face it: You're a small business

---

[1] September 2012 report from Valassis and RedPlum, www.marketingcharts.com/wp/direct/us-consumers-willing-to-get-social-for-deals-23182.

owner, not an online marketing guru. And that's *okay*. You've gotten as far as you have in your business by focusing on what you know, and honing your area of expertise. You don't have to be an expert in using online resources, because this book is going to help you with that. We'll show you how to easily apply a few key marketing principles to your business so that you can concentrate on being the amazing small business owner that you are—and feel like a marketing guru at the same time.

You also don't have to be a client of my company, Demandforce, to get value out of reading this book. My intent is to give all small business owners the tools they need in order to quickly build an effective plan aimed at converting online shoppers into offline customers. It will be easy for you to put this plan into action, and it will deliver impressive results for your business. The chapters ahead contain tips and tricks, worksheets, and best practices that we teach our customers every day to compliment the Demandforce program. This information will help *you* get that much closer to "wild success."

A LITTLE BIT ABOUT DEMANDFORCE

Since 2003, Demandforce has worked closely with well over 30,000 small- and medium-sized businesses across the United States, Canada, and the UK to uncover the "secret ingredient" needed to run and grow a thriving business. As a result, we've managed to effectively implement the two key factors that are missing from most traditional marketing plans:

1. Empowering small business owners with the time to deliver killer experiences and build strong relationships with customers
2. Leveraging the power of the Internet and social media to convert those trusted relationships into recommendations and referrals

We've found that small business owners can accomplish these by taking several specific actions: utilizing easy, turnkey solutions for decreasing no-show rates and increasing repeat business; targeting their marketing conversation; and leveraging a consistent stream of syndicated, consumer-generated review content. This approach allows owners to refocus their energy on delivering exceptional service experiences that continue to fuel the cycle.

Our core focus has always been on services-based professionals, such as doctors, hair stylists, veterinarians, dentists, auto shop professionals, and so forth. In April 2012, we were acquired by Intuit to be offered as the front-office business solution for its 4 million QuickBooks customers. Since then, we've welcomed small business owners from a multitude of historically underserved services-based industries—including plumbers, electricians, gardeners, and more—to the Demandforce family. It's been an absolute pleasure learning from these businesses and providing them with business solutions that really affect their bottom line, and we're thrilled to share some of their secrets to success with you in this book.

CHAPTER 1

Understanding and Connecting with the Connected Consumer

Before we jump into the nitty-gritty of building your online marketing plan, let's first spend a few minutes understanding your target audience. No matter where in the world your business is located, there will always be an increasingly important segment of your target audience that you need to tap into—a group we call *Connected Consumers*.

WHO IS THE CONNECTED CONSUMER?

There are two common ways to describe the so-called Connected Consumer. One definition refers to how savvy they are with mobile technology. These individuals typically browse for products and services on their mobile devices and frequently consume media through several outlets at once (e.g., uploading a photo to Facebook while surfing the web on their tablets or laptops while also watching a television show). They also have a tendency to search for prices on their mobile devices before they buy a new product, potentially while they're staring at the product while in the store. When it comes to recommendations, the Connected Consumer's opinion tends to hold more weight within social circles. He or she is often the first person his or her friends approach for an opinion on whether they should buy a given item, or for a recommendation on a good service provider.

But there's a second newer and more relevant definition of the Connected Consumer—one that extends the notion of mobility and refers to that person's overall *social connectedness*, combined with his or her *willingness to share* through online social platforms. This person

1

takes pictures of his or her purchases to share with friends online and isn't afraid to let the world know what he or she is doing right now, and with whom. Socially Connected Consumers don't just "check in" somewhere; they're likely also telling their friends about their absolute favorite dish at your restaurant or a to-die-for hair treatment from your salon that they can't live without. Socially Connected Consumers use their social networks to actively volunteer information about businesses where they spend their money. As a result, they can become activists for your business after just one purchase experience.

The key differentiation between these two definitions is that the Socially Connected Consumer is *actively marketing* your business for you when they publish their experiences on their social networks—often without you ever asking them to—while the traditional Connected Consumer plays a much more passive role. Mobile connectivity is often a tool for added convenience for the latter group. While they are happy to recommend products or services, they are likely asked for their opinions before they go out of their way to share them.

In order to flourish, small businesses must effectively utilize the Socially Connected Consumer's active willingness to share. In today's connected economy, this is the one of the key differences between a merely healthy business and wildly successful one.

MORE CONNECTED CONSUMERS THAN EVER

In his 1962 book *Diffusion of Innovations*, author and communication scholar Everett Rogers popularized his theory of the "innovation adoption curve"—the rate at which society adopts new trends, technologies, or ideas. Rogers and his colleagues believed that in order for the innovation to be lasting, it had to reach critical mass and be widely adopted. Social media adoption within the U.S., as well as the rate of most other technologies, follows the adoption curve illustrated in Figure 1.1.

In fact, it was 2011 that really marked the shift to critical mass social media adoption in the United States, which represents the shift from Early Majority to Late Majority in the adoption curve. This was when more than 50 percent of the U.S. population was joining social media platforms *en masse* to engage and connect. Consumer research firms Edison Research and Arbitron released a study in May 2011 at the

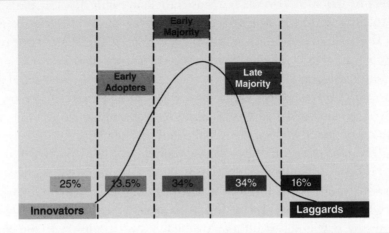

FIGURE 1.1   Rate of Adoption across Society for Ideas, Trends, and Technology

Blogworld East conference entitled "The Social Habit,"[1] which points to this shift to critical mass:

- 88 percent of U.S. residents have Internet access at home.
- Globally, 52 percent of people ages 21 and over have a profile on one or more social networking sites, up from 48 percent in 2010.
- In the United States, 76 percent of people are members of at least one social networking site.
- 2011 marked tremendous growth in social networking adoption for the 35 and over population.
- 79 percent of those on social networks update their statuses at least once per week.

Of course, it's hard to ignore the elephant in the room. Facebook represented the majority of this dataset; over 400 million people (58 percent of the user base at the time of the Edison Research publication) were using the social media platform on a daily basis. While other popular social platforms like LinkedIn and Twitter did grow their membership

---

[1] Edison Research published presentation, May 29, 2011, www.slideshare.net/webby 2001/the-social-habit-2011-by-edison-research.

counts in 2011, Facebook stands as the clear winner and as the social platform driving mass adoption.

The numbers are even more staggering in 2012. There were more than 800 million people on major social platforms, and a Pew Internet Survey confirms that in 2012, 61 percent of adults under 30 used a social networking site at least once a day. With Internet users between the ages of 50 and 64, social media usage rose sharply to 32 percent from 20 percent the previous year.[2]

That said, there are several social platforms that may be more or less relevant for your business. Depending on your target market, you may want to consider LinkedIn as your primary focus. Accountants, legal consultants, financial advisors, and other professional services–related businesses may find that this professional network delivers on the ability to build a stronger connection with their customers and followers than any other social networking site. These markets may also find it more

---

Socially Connected Consumer versus Social Influencer

The key difference between a Socially Connected Consumer and Social Influencer is that the second person will use pretty much any medium to communicate his or her recommendations—and it doesn't matter which one he or she chooses. When a Social Influencer passionately advocates a product or service, he or she creates a trend wave that friends and followers readily jump on.

Leveraging Social Influencers isn't about finding a celebrity to adore your product or service and tweet about it. Social Influencers exist across all of the social groups noted in Rogers's innovation adoption model (see Figure 1.1). For many small businesses, converting a small but vocal group of loyal Social Influencers creates a strong foundation for long-term growth. In Chapters 8 and 9, we'll explore some topics around incentivizing and rewarding both your Socially Connected Consumers and those coveted Social Influencers.

---

[2]Worldwide Social Media Usage Trends in 2012, http://searchenginewatch.com/article/2167518/Worldwide-Social-Media-Usage-Trends-in-2012.

compelling to focus on LinkedIn given that 71 percent of that network's users have obtained four-year college degrees (as opposed to 41 percent of those on Facebook),[3] and may therefore have a higher likelihood to need their services.

Most businesses aren't sure which social platforms are right for them starting off; initially, you're just looking to get the biggest return on investment through social channels. To get a better feel for your customer base, you should focus your social strategy on testing some of the easy-to-implement and low-cost marketing programs we discuss in later chapters. Don't put all your eggs in one basket if you don't know what's going to work; it's perfectly okay and, actually, a much better idea to test and see which programs will allow you to reach your target segment most effectively.

CONNECTING WITH THE SOCIALLY CONNECTED CONSUMER

Though the strategy is simple: Make it as easy and attractive as possible for Socially Connected Consumers to interact with your business in their everyday lives. Executing this plan, however, can seem overwhelming.

The upcoming chapters will discuss specific programs you can implement *today* to bring in a sustainable number of customers to promote healthy growth for your business. In the meantime, keep the following key considerations in mind when thinking about how you're going to execute your strategy.

It Still Starts with Search

You may not think of an Internet search as being particularly social; however, it's come a long way since Alta Vista and the early Yahoo! incarnations of the 1990s. Socially Connected Consumers not only have their preferences for social networks, but they are also actively using search engines for products and services across the web. In the United States today, Google dominates the search ecosystem, owning just over 70 percent of the search results on the web, with Yahoo! and Bing working to gain market share. The trick is for businesses to understand

---

[3] The Social Habit 2012 Report, http://socialhabit.com/secure/wp-content/uploads/2012/07/The-Social-Habit-2012-by-Edison-Research.pdf.

which search terms your potential customers are using to find you online. Showing up in the first few pages of the search results for your industry, specialty, and geographic location is critical to converting online browsers to offline customers.

Competition is fierce for high placement in organic search results. However, there are several no-cost tactics you can implement today to optimize your online presence and give your website the best chance of displaying well in organic search results. (We discuss these in more detail in Chapters 2 and 3.)

Can I Get Away with Not Paying for Search Placement?

This is a decision you're going to need to make for yourself and your business. Although it may not be an option in every market, it's possible that if you correctly optimize your website, search engines across the board will rank you higher. If you do this well, you may actually find better results with this approach than you would by paying for Search Engine Optimization (SEO), or paying for higher placement in search results, placement with single search engines like Google or Bing.

Keeping everything that's within your control accurate and consistent is your goal here. We'll discuss how you can impact each of the top three key factors for organic search ranking in Chapter 3.

Keep Your Home Tidy on the Web

When it comes to making it as easy as possible for anyone to find your business, you must meet a minimum threshold for an acceptable website before Socially Connected Consumers will deem your business worth their time and potentially convert to an offline sale. Your business website should have a clean, modern feel that serves the primary purpose of delivering to the casual browser the information they need to become a buyer. You'd be surprised at how many businesses don't have the basics like business hours, physical address, phone number, and contact email address front and center on their websites. Countless others set up websites but fail to enable online reviews and customer testimonials or to provide an easy way for browsers to request service. Chapters 2 and 3 discuss several other strategies for keeping your website focused on converting shoppers to buyers, as well as provide basics for how to optimize your website for search results.

Which Social Networks Do My Customers Frequent?

There are dozens of social networks you may want to consider, depending on the type of service or product your business sells. Highly specialized directories and sites come in and out of fashion fairly regularly with Socially Connected Consumers, so it's not always the best idea to hop on the latest bandwagon.

That said, it's a pretty safe bet, given Facebook's staggering adoption numbers, that many of your customers log on to this site at least once a month, and probably use the mobile app on their smart phones regularly. The benefits for businesses are built into Facebook's several "share friendly" platform mechanisms, giving you easy access to your customers' networks. For example, once Facebook opened their developer API, or application programming interface—the programming specification for businesses to build applications and easily "plug into" Facebook—in 2007, the social network quickly evolved into a platform that welcomed businesses to leverage the data Facebook already had on its users for their benefit, and vice versa. Features like username authentication to comment on a blog, logging in to an account to update your online preferences, and sending a photo or deal to a friend all became easy and seamless parts of the Facebook ecosystem. For small businesses, a "like" for your blog or website could now be syndicated on that person's Facebook feed, automatically and instantaneously spreading the word about your service to all of your customer's friends. Tools like these make it simpler than you might think to convert an online review, uploaded photo, tagged friend, or location check-in into a referral engine.

Another consumer review platform to consider is Yelp. Because this site has a loyal following as an online business directory, especially in the major U.S. metro areas, it makes sense to put some focus here. In fact, if you've been in business for over a year or are located in a larger metropolitan area, it's likely you already have a profile on Yelp, and it's something that you may want to claim and monitor as a part of your online marketing strategy.

Other specialty sites and directories to consider include Google+ Local, Yahoo! Local, Bing Local, CitySearch, Angie's List, TripAdvisor, InsiderPages, OpenTable, JudysBook, and, of course, Demandforce. Depending on your industry, you may also already have a microsite on these directories that you should consider claiming to make sure your business is accurately represented.

What Is My Budget?

In 2012, Staples conducted their sixth annual Staples National Small Business Survey, during which they asked the American Consumer Opinion's panel about their plans for spending in the upcoming year. Sixty-seven percent of small business owners with 20 or fewer employees stated that they planned on spending just over $2,000 on marketing in 2012.[4]

It can be intimidating to think that you need to compete for visibility online against companies spending millions in marketing annually when your total marketing budget is in the low thousands. This is why small businesses need to think specifically about budget in terms of both money *and* time. This is an instance in which the "time is money" adage never rang more true. For example, you might have relatively little money to spend, but you can invest five to seven hours per week in executing your marketing plan. This seems to be the most common scenario for small business owners—as well as the most ideal. And if you have employees to whom you can delegate certain tasks related to your marketing plan, you're in even better shape.

Quality over Quantity

Selecting your core channels, as well as overall frequency of communication, should always be a consideration. Your goal through social and online channels is to reach the right customers at the right time without oversaturating your audience. Putting too much out there too quickly lends to a more disconnected customer base and a higher rate of people who choose to opt out from receiving communications from your business.

Starting small also gives you a much more realistic idea of the actual long-term time and dollar commitment you're making. It's most important to provide consistent frequency and quality of engagement with customers through online social channels. For now, posting once or twice a week on social networks is just fine.

---

[4]Staples National Small Business Survey, http://staples.newshq.businesswire.com/press-release/corporate/staples-gives-small-businesses-push-250000-free-advertising.

This Bed Fits Just Right

Goldilocks knew what she was talking about. It's important to create the right balance for your marketing plan, finding the sweet spot between too much and too little. Overcommitting your resources in order to execute your plan means that you're probably taking away from something else that's potentially more important. And bringing in too much business too fast can be just as detrimental as never having started!

TIP—Get to Know Your Customers

If you have no idea where to start when it comes to identifying the social networks that your customers frequent, we recommend that you provide an incentive for the customers who are already coming through your doors to fill out a small survey. Offer your customers 10 percent or $15 off their next purchase as an easy way to get some additional information and to ensure a return visit.

Keep an inexpensive tablet at the register with a survey already pulled up in the browser and ready to go. (You can create free surveys at surveymonkey.com.) That way, you don't have to deal with organizing and then analyzing your results; you can show your customers how tech savvy you are and you can make their lives easier by simply handing them the tablet to complete the survey while you ring up their purchases. If you have an online shopping site, you can similarly gather information from your buyers by offering a coupon during or after the checkout process for filling in additional information. Alternatively, you can also include your questions during or after the online checkout process. Make sure that you are monitoring for cart abandonment if you are making data collection a part of the online purchase experience, as too many fields to fill out will cause buyers to drop off at an increased rate. You may need to test over time to figure out how much is too much for your online customers. Make sure to give your survey takers a coupon code for their next purchase so you can track usage and return rate.

(continued)

(*continued*)

Keep your survey short enough for customers to complete during the cashier transaction. Here's a list of sample survey questions worth asking:

When you search for businesses like this online, what sites do you use? Select all applicable:

- Google
- Yelp
- Facebook
- Bing
- Yahoo!
- JudysBook
- InsiderPages
- Angie's List
- CitySearch
- Other: _____

When you think of businesses like this, what kinds of search terms would you use online to find us? [Select a few examples that are relevant to your business category.]

- Garden supplies city/state
- Local jewelry
- Go-kart racing
- Other: _____

How did you find us today?

- Referral from existing customer
- Walking through the neighborhood
- I found you online
- Other: _____

What social networks/websites do you frequent, if any?

- Facebook
- MySpace
- Foursquare

- Digg
- Tumblr
- Pinterest
- YouTube
- LinkedIn
- Other: _____

Would you ever visit our website or Facebook page for special offers to redeem in-store?

- Yes
- No

Have you ever written an online review about a business?

- Yes, regularly
- Yes, but not frequently
- No, and I don't plan to

We're considering emailing special offers about once a month to our customers. If you would like to receive these special offers, please provide your contact information below:

- First Name: _____
- Last Name: _____
- Email: _____

Data like this is extremely valuable. It will give you a more accurate understanding of where your customers are spending their time online, where and how they search, and whether they are good candidates for being your online referral engines in the future. If you're considering investing in online advertising, you'll have a much better idea of which websites they visit most frequently, and with which search terms you want to consider buying placement.

No two businesses are identical, and the same holds true for customers that frequent those businesses. If you don't have the time or inclination to both collect and use data from

(continued)

(*continued*)

your customers to better understand them, it's perfectly fine to start by using more generic customer segmentations for your marketing plan. However, you'll eventually want to learn about your customers' habits so that you can focus your marketing and continue to engage with the right people. Even if you choose not to have a survey, definitely opt for an email signup sheet so you can at least collect email addresses. Building a database of opted-in email addresses is often the biggest challenge for small business owners, so the earlier you start asking for email addresses, and the more consistently you continue to ask, the better! You can download an offline form you can use at your register here: www.wiley.com/go/small bizhandbook (Download A).

Today's social economy is truly an opportunity for small businesses to accelerate growth and establish lasting reputations in a way that has never been possible before. Socially Connected Consumers want to participate in building your business and will celebrate your successes as if they were their own. They're proud of being the first ones to find you and spread the word on your behalf. On the sobering side, your greatest evangelists will also hold you accountable for your mistakes in an excruciatingly public manner, but they will be equally as public when you strive to make things right, which creates a win–win situation for everyone. Socially Connected Consumers can be your most valuable feet on the street, and we'll discuss throughout this book strategies for identifying and leveraging this segment of your customer base.

CHAPTER 2

Building a Plan for Your Small Business's Online Reputation

Although the idea of planning can be daunting, it can also be a fun and relatively easy exercise for you and your business—really! It's not critical that you follow whatever plan you develop precisely; however, it *is* crucial to take a serious look at the state of your online reputation as it exists today, so you can assess how much work you need to do.

The process of building and mapping this plan is intended to give you some perspective on how your online reputation looks today, to help you understand whether you will have the bandwidth to manage your online reputation, and to help you effectively communicate your needs if you *do* need to find some help. Remember, you don't always need outside help, and you can do most of this yourself if you really want to. Also remember that no matter how mature your online presence is, there's always room to improve it.

You can approach this next section as you would while building a salad at the salad bar. You have the base necessities; you then just need to select which extras you want to make it just right for you.

IDENTIFY YOUR STARTING POINT

Most small businesses will be at some stage other than the very beginning, even if they haven't actively done anything on the web for their business profile or to increase awareness for their business online. With so many business directories online these days, it's probable that at least one of them has matched your physical address and business information to create a skeleton profile for you online. Therefore, a good place to start is to visit each of the following websites using the search parameters: Full Business Name, Phone Number (with area code), and Physical Address (including zip code). We've provided example scenarios of what you might commonly find.

	Search Parameter		
	Full Business Name	*Phone Number*	*Physical Address*
Google.com	Two Google business profiles matched, need to merge	Two Google business profiles matched, need to merge	One Google business match, the other has the old address
Bing.com	No business profile—need to create	One match, different business	No business profile—need to create
Yelp.com	One profile match, incorrect info—need to claim	Two profile matches, incorrect info—need to claim	One profile match, incorrect info—need to claim
CitySearch .com	None, need to create	One match, different business	None, need to create
Facebook .com	One business match	One business match	One business match
Yahoo.com	Two profiles, need to merge	Two profiles, need to merge	Two profiles, need to merge

Let's say as an example that you found on Google.com that your business displayed two profile results with for the same Phone Number and on CitySearch.com your business displayed two profile results with different Physical Addresses but the same phone number after completing this exercise for your business (it's not uncommon for different directories to display very different results). A few things stand out as items you need to address for the foundation of your online reputation plan. First, it's clear that the business's phone number used to be someone else's, and that search engines have indexed that phone number with the old business. You can simply correct this by reporting the error to each site (don't worry, it's easy to do). Second, it seems that the business changed locations at some point, something that you also need to correct with each site (and another easily accomplished task).

Third, if a directory has two or more profiles for your business, you need to request to have these merged into a single profile (this *can* be easy, depending on the site). Though it's fairly common to see multiple profiles for a single business, it's crucial to claim and merge these into a single entity. By doing so, you reduce confusion for potential shoppers, encourage existing customers to write reviews for you on the correct page, and reduce the amount of administrative work you need to conduct to monitor and manage your online reputation over time.

Websites update their help and FAQ sections and change processes very frequently. Therefore, we won't go into the details of how to perform these tasks with each site, as this information could very well be outdated by tomorrow. If you do come upon one of these issues, I recommend that you first visit your actual business profile page on that website. Then log in, claim the page (if you haven't done this yet, there's usually a big button toward the top of the page that says "Claim This Page" or "Own This Business? Click Here"), and report the error directly from the business profile page.

Why Do I Have Multiple Profiles?

I know it seems strange to uncover various online profiles for your business, especially if you never knew they existed to begin with. The reality is that online directories get information from various sources: businesses create pages themselves; syndication partners such as Demandforce feed directories data about local businesses; and directories themselves may scrape the web for physical address matches and set up unverified skeleton pages for higher search results. In addition, consumers might even check-in at your business to automatically generate a page, or create pages themselves on your behalf. With all of these different variables at play, it's not unlikely that more than one profile exists for your business in any of the major business directories online. Regardless of how the profile page came to exist, it's your job to make sure that you work with those sites to correct the situation if you do find an error and verify the profile's content for accuracy.

Understanding your starting point will give you a clear picture of how much work you need to do to manage your online reputation. Some businesses have very complex situations that might require them to involve a professional. An example of a more complex scenario that happened with one of our clients was when the business hired a third-party firm to increase their new customer acquisition rates, and the third-party firm created a new phone number and designed an entirely new website in order to increase the business' chances for higher page ranking on search engines (this practice is generally not condoned by search engine marketers). Although the business was just a single entity, it acted like two completely separate businesses online so search engines had a difficult time with knowing what to do with the information being fed for matching and as a result had to undergo a very lengthy—and expensive—process of untangling the mess. If you're lucky, you've got a fairly clean slate—just a few single profile matches here and there. You can simply claim these on your business's behalf and move on to tackling the core components of your online reputation plan.

START BY TAKING A MINIMALISTIC APPROACH: CORE COMPONENTS

If you only have a few precious hours a month to focus on managing your online reputation, this minimalistic approach is the best one for you to take. There are three core elements to this approach: ensuring your business information is accurate, updating your website, and simple monitoring. These serve as the foundation for your online reputation. When a potential customer searches for the product or service you offer online, search engines need to have accurate business information to match you with search results. Then, when a consumer tries to actually find you, you want to make sure you've provided accurate details regarding your location across the web and that you have already addressed anything potentially negative out there.

Accurate Business Information

Search engines have a particularly difficult time matching businesses with relevant profiles in search results when there are inconsistencies in your business information. Even a seemingly insignificant discrepancy (such as your website showing your physical address as 123 Casey Blvd. versus 123 Casey Boulevard) can cause problems. Make sure that every online entity you manage displays your necessary business information—business name, physical address, business phone number, business email address, and website URL—in *exactly the same way*. Having variations in your primary business information might mean that you have multiple pages under the same business name, creating confusion for your prospective customers and making it more difficult for you to manage your online presence.

It's critical for businesses like Demandforce, which syndicates fresh business information and reviews across the web as a part of our service, to use primary business information that always matches exactly. This allows our syndication partners to automatically connect this valuable content to the correct profile. In fact, the most common reason that reviews and business information don't make it to the right profile page is that the business name, physical address, or business phone number did not match exactly. If there are multiple profiles for the business, this also often keeps the directory from being able to identify the right page when making algorithmic recommendations to consumers who are simply browsing their directory site.

Your Home on the Web: Your Business Website

Think of your business website as your online homestead. Everything about your website should tell a story about what your business is and, in some ways, who *you are* as a business owner. This site needs to convey reliable, accurate, and up-to-date information. It should have a prominently displayed mailbox that allows browsers to easily get in touch with you if they want to. It should also have a trouble-free way for those potential customers to read testimonials or reviews about the service or products you provide, and give those same people a way to become offline customers. Most importantly, your website needs to have the right *keywords* (and enough of them) located throughout the main and secondary site pages to ensure that you'll rank in the first few pages when prospective customers are searching for what you offer.

Lets break each of these topics down a little further.

The Basic Information   Make sure your business name, physical location (city and state included), phone number, business hours, and email address, as well as a link to directions to your location, are available on the sidebar, header, or footer of every page on your website in a consistent location. In addition, make sure every page on your website is titled. Many websites are using a structure that looks like this: Business Name | Service Description in City, State (and/or Neighborhood) | Page Title. You can use your website builder tool to edit your page titles. If you build your own HTML pages, you can add the <title> tag to the <head> section of the code.

Figure 2.1 is an example of an effective title tag and how it shows up in your browser search results. When searching for "San Francisco dentist," Demandforce customer Green Dentistry often comes up near the top of search results.

The title tag is both general enough for someone willing to travel a bit and specific enough (with a zip code) for someone looking for a dentist specific to his or her neighborhood. It's great that the tag includes both the city and the zip code designations, as you never know which will be used to search.

You should also include in the basics a way for prospective customers to reach out to you. If you don't have a ready-made online form to use, you can easily create one by utilizing one of several website building tools. Then, you just have this information emailed to you each time someone submits the form. If you have an online form to gather quote or appointment requests (or email addresses to join your mailing list), show that on each page as well. For instance, Demandforce customers can drop the ready-made scheduler widget into most website tools and have requests submit directly to your Demandforce account.

Tell Your Story   Small business is personal, so you should make your online presence personal. Show off the fact that you're a local business, and don't be afraid to tell your story to prospective buyers who visit

---

Family Dentist | **Green Dentistry** | San Francisco, CA 94108

FIGURE 2.1   Google Search Result—"San Francisco Dentist"

your site. Make sure you have an About Us, or Company Information page in your main table of contents that includes photos of the founders and details on why this business exists today. Upload a video that includes a tour of the business or interviews with employees. Show prospective customers the kind of fantastic service they can expect from you.

If your business has ever received press or blog coverage, include that as well. Even if your friend posted a glowing review about you to a blog that she simply writes as a hobby, link to this post from your website. Make your business look as attractive as possible, and take advantage of the free press. If you are selling products that are hard to find in your local area, make sure to link to the external corporate site for those product lines so online browsers can get the information they need to make a purchase decision. As well, for every online directory that you've chosen to focus your marketing time on, make sure you're linking your business website to those pages. Linking to relevant external sites is an important part of online marketing, and improves your search results placement over time.

If you have evolved into delivering services or products that you consider more niche than general, be sure to highlight these offerings throughout your website. Use text, in addition to images, so specific keywords and phrases get picked up by search engines. Take the time to describe your business practices in detail, including associations you've joined to represent your niche market. Then, communicate your passion about why you've chosen to focus your energy here.

Testimonials Are Key Past reviews from customers paint a picture of what it's like to do business with your company and are perhaps the most important conversion tool you can have on your website. Make sure to have a page dedicated to reviews and testimonials if you're building your own website. You can go the straightforward route and label it "Reviews" or "Testimonials" or get creative with something like "Why Buy from Us." Include photos, if you can get permission from your happy reviewers, to highlight the personal nature of your interactions with them.

A great review or testimonial is short and sweet, but still tells the story of a positive interaction with your company. Anything from 15 to 150 words is ideal. Going over that runs the risk of having potential customers gloss over your content, which lessens its impact. Making it too short usually means that content lacks enough depth to be worth placing on your site.

There are two basic kinds of reviews. The first speaks to the more emotional nature of the experience and delivers insight to potential buyers about what it "feels like" to be a patron of this business. Here are a few examples of great "emotion driven" reviews:

I visited [xxxx] on recommendation of a friend. My current dentist was certainly not bad, but certainly not exciting! So, the prospect of actually enjoying a trip to "any" doctor (as my friend suggested) was appealing. She was right. Everyone was engaging, asked questions, offered feedback, remembered my story and passed it on to the next person whom I interacted with. And, they all smiled!

A man who listens is a wonderful thing. . . and Jason is just such a man. I wasn't looking for a big change, just wanted to get my long hair trimmed; he gave me just what I wanted, only 10,000 times better than I ever expected. The best haircut of my life; looking forward to the next time with anticipation rather than the usual trepidation. Yea, Jason!

I had an excellent experience and so did my dog. The staff was friendly and efficient and more importantly on time. My dog did not want to leave! I would highly recommend [xxxx].

There is something special about these kinds of emotionally driven reviews. They often speak to the connection the customer had with the business or service provider, whether it be enabling the customer to enjoy a typically unenjoyable service, having his or her expectations for a simple task wildly exceeded, or creating an environment that makes the customer's beloved pet so happy it doesn't want to leave. A really great review of this type makes the reader want that very same experience.

The second type of review is more informational. These reviews tend to be a little longer, but provide specific details about the experience that other potential buyers can benefit from knowing in advance. Here's an example of a review I recently wrote for a local breakfast spot in San Carlos, California—My Breakfast House:

Extra crispy hash browns.

Serving sizes were actually reasonable.

French toast was how I like it—deep in eggy batter.

Pancakes were fluffy and filled with big, juicy blueberries.

Grapefruit juice was ice cold.

I love that there's a dedicated kid's playroom. It's a tiny room off the dining area and parents and families come here to eat while the little ones play to their hearts' content. Just brilliant. I can't wait to do the same.

Restaurants, resorts, spas, and other menu-based businesses, in particular, benefit from these kinds of more informational reviews because they often provide recommendations on the best dishes or services to try on the menu. Informational reviews serve a secondary purpose because the text is fully searchable on these review sites. Oftentimes, those searching for a restaurant are looking to fulfill a specific craving, so the more detail there is on specific dishes reviewers loved, the better.

Include Educational Information An often overlooked but important piece of a business website is additional material that can help consumers make informed decisions. There are two big benefits to including lots of interesting external reference materials for your prospective buyers. First, you can think of externally referenced educational content as additional testimonials for your product or service. Try to find online articles by trusted sources that emphasize your offering's benefits. For instance, if you're selling a specific lip gloss for a reason, then link to a magazine article that highlights that lip gloss. Or, if you're an auto shop that focuses on a specific type of hybrid technology because you're passionate about it, link to some articles that reinforce your passion. By providing prospective buyers with external references that reinforce the purchase decision, you are potentially speeding up their decision-making process. Be sure to include relevant snippets from these external sites, so not everyone has to leave your site if they want to get an idea of the content.

Second, websites with more complex external linking strategies tend to rank higher in search results. SEO companies may approach your business over the years and offer their services for building links throughout your site. You don't necessarily need to take advantage of this; it's certainly something you can take on yourself, but there *is* some work involved. It's not something you can "set and forget." There's no need to go overboard focusing on SEO here. However, you do want to regularly update your links to ensure they are "live" (they work), and you want to be adding current content as you find it. A broken link is worse than no link at all. In addition, keep in mind that three links from five years ago will not cut it here—for search engines *or* your prospective customers. I recommend that you empower one of your employees who is interested in learning about online marketing and let him own the task of keeping your website content updated.

A very underutilized but equally important way to increase credibility with prospective clients is for the business to share educational information with the public about the business of doing business. In doing so, the business can be seen as deeply engrained in the professional community, as a thought leader, and as a business that believes in giving back. As shown in Figure 2.2, Festoon Salon in the San Francisco Bay area makes it a point to share their expertise in how to run a salon, train team members, and manage the operational back end of the business.

Keywords and Descriptions Having the right keywords and descriptions can be a key differentiator when it comes to search results. Web crawlers scour the Internet for text content on websites that is exact

FIGURE 2.2   Festoon Saloon Training Page

and for contextual matches to the phrases that people enter into search engines. Depending on the quality of the match, your website can potentially display much higher in search results. While it's important to understand how this works as a baseline for why the right keywords and descriptions are an important piece of your website, you also want to make sure the core of your strategy here serves the purpose of delivering information to your prospective customers.

Determining which keywords are relevant for your business is a little bit of an art. You can start by completing this exercise:

- On a blank sheet of paper, list all of the categories that you've ever listed yourself under in business directories. For instance, someone who fixes air conditioners may have listed his or her business under HVAC, air conditioning, heating, home improvement, home services, and so forth.
- Ask a few friends how they would look for this information: "If your air conditioner broke or you were in the market for a new heater or duct cleaning, what would you search for online?" You might hear things like: central heating, digital thermometer installation, air conditioner installation, AC repair, HVAC, duct cleaner, fix broken heater, heater igniter replacement, new heater quote, and so on.
- Take a look at your product or service portfolio. List name brands that might stand out for consumers, as well as any colloquial terms for the products and services sold, like *aircon* versus *air conditioning*.
- Consolidate these notes into a single list of the top 10 to 15 terms that are the most relevant to your business. This is your first keywords list.

Your next step is to find ways to integrate these keywords into your website's text content. You may also want to repeat the top keywords on secondary site pages as well. For the most part, this won't be difficult. Remember, your website's primary purpose is to make sure you have enough (but not too much) information to convert prospective shoppers into customers. You want to maintain a 60:40 ratio of text to images so as not to overwhelm your visitors.

With the previous search for "San Francisco dentist," let's see how Google did with keyword matches on the website. As shown in Figure 2.3, the text content on the main page of the business's website includes text matches for the search results, which lends to the search algorithm as

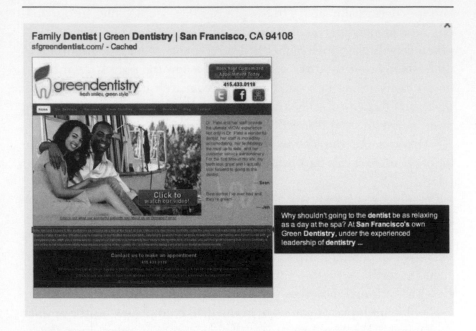

FIGURE 2.3   Green Dentistry Google Search Results Preview

well. In addition, the keywords used in this search are scattered on the other pages throughout the website which also helps with search results placement.

This website is particularly appealing to search engines because almost all of the text is searchable, including the menu bar at the top, as opposed to being embedded in images. So when a consumer is searching for something more specific like a "green certified dentist in San Francisco," Dr. Patel's website is at the top of the search results (see Figures 2.4). Once you hover over Green Dentistry's link in Google, a results preview will display (shown in Figure 2.5) which highlights specifically where on the main website page your requested search terms are located. The more searchable text with relevant keywords you have throughout your website, the better your chances of getting found by online shoppers through search engines.

Remember, your website's primary purpose is to make sure you have enough (but not too much) information to convert prospective shoppers into customers. Images are an important part of creating a visually attractive website, but make sure you have enough text for

Green Certified | Family Dentist | Green Dentistry | San Francisco ...
sfgreendentist.com/green-certified/
Going **green** isn't just good for the planet, it's good for our patients. **San Francisco
Green Dentistry** is a LEED **Certified Green** practice dedicated to keeping you ...

Family Dentist | Green Dentistry | San Francisco, CA 94108
sfgreendentist.com/
Dr. Nammy Patel is a family **dentist in San Francisco**, CA offering services as a Cerec
& invisalign **dentist** and providing cosmetic **dentistry**, teeth whitening, ...
Score: **24** / 30 - 21 Google reviews - Write a review

 360 Post St #704 San Francisco, CA 94108
(415) 433-0119

FIGURE 2.4   Green Dentistry Google Search Results

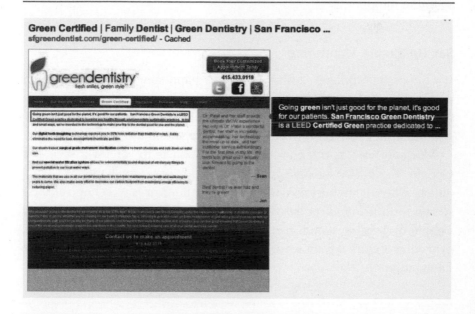

FIGURE 2.5   Green Dentistry Google Search Results Preview

search engines to crawl and use for search results matching. As we
mentioned, maintain a 60:40 ratio of text to images so you don't to
overwhelm those visiting your site.

Your objective in managing core components of your online reputation is twofold: (1) to make sure you have enough information so

prospective customers can find you online when they perform more general searches, and (2) to make sure you've made your business as attractive as possible to convert offline customers when they get there. This will be a work in progress throughout the life of your business. Even if you only have a few hours a month, you should focus on building and maintaining your online reputation.

Remember, your website is your homestead on the web. It needs to be an effective advertisement on its own for your business. Even if you never post a single promotion on your website, you still need to provide enough relevant content (business information, your story, product/service highlights, and so on, as discussed earlier) to convert browsers to customers on the merits of your business alone. Even in this "shopper's economy," you don't need to always offer a discount in order to convert an online shopper.

Set Up Simple Monitoring

It's impossible to keep abreast of what's happening on the web at all times; there's simply too much to keep up with. Thankfully, there are free and easy-to-use tools out there to help you monitor the web for potentially negative sentiment, reviews, or content.

An easy way to track online conversation is to set up a series of Google Alerts (www.google.com/alerts). This way, you'll receive daily emails when your business name, your name, or any other relevant search term is found on the web. As you create each alert, you'll see a sample of possible search results, helping you hone your search terms over time. Figure 2.6 shows an example of two Google Alerts set up for Demandforce.

Alerts

Everything	Volume	How often	Deliver to	
Annie Tsai	Only the best results	Once a day		Edit
demandforce	All results	Once a day		Edit

FIGURE 2.6   Google Alerts Sample

A VERY CLOSE SECOND: MANAGE PRIMARY
BUSINESS AND SOCIAL DIRECTORIES

Depending on where your business is geographically, your list of primary online directories may vary. In major metro areas throughout the United States, for example, social networking plays a much larger role in determining an online directory's popularity. Therefore, local business sites like Google, Yahoo!, and Bing find themselves up against the likes of Yelp and Foursquare when fighting for the top three spots. And in Europe, Foursquare leads the social pack for trusted recommendations and check-ins.

Based on your geographic location, identify the top three online directories consumers use when they're searching for the products and services you offer. If you don't know where to start, use the survey data that you gathered in Chapter 1 to get a better picture of this information. Then, make sure you do the following with each of the top three directories:

- Claim your business page and address any issues you find.
- Verify the accuracy of the core business information on this page (name, address, contact information, services offered, etc.).
- Add photos, a business description, and so forth that tell a story about your business to potential buyers.
- Comment on or address any existing public reviews that need attention.

Once you have these things in order, you're in a great position to monitor and then interact as time permits. The value you'll get out of engaging with customers and prospective customers through these online reputation outlets depends entirely on the quality of that engagement. As with most ventures, you will get out what you put in. However, there are some high-impact actions you can take to make the most of your time. We'll discuss these next.

HAVE EXTRA TIME? DO MORE: THE BENEFITS OF INTEGRATING
VISUAL AND SOCIAL MEDIA INTO YOUR ONLINE PRESENCE

These days, taking full ownership of your online reputation requires that you do much more than manage a static profile on a business directory.

Not only do social profiles increase your business's visibility when it comes to organic search results with major search engines, but they also serve as secondary landing pages—think "live" websites. As such, they can give you the opportunity to present a more personal side to your business that you otherwise may not be able to do.

While not everyone has the bandwidth to go that extra step and actively manage their social presences, the following are some easy ways to make a big impact when it comes to visual and social media.

Make It Personal with Visual Media

The old saying that "a picture is worth a thousand words" rings true when it comes to pictures that move as well. Your objective in regards to visual media should be to put faces to names, to put people in front of your brand, and to give meaning to words. It's been shown that a Facebook status update with a photo and a caption generates around four times more engagement than text alone does, and one that incorporates video shows even more success, with an average of six times more engagement. Of course, context is the most important thing, so make sure the video content is appropriate for the channel and your audience. We'll spend some time talking about how to create videos for social channels in Chapter 8.

It's hard to ignore the value of the right photo or video gallery. Here are a few tips to getting the most of your investment here, whether it's time or money:

- **Introduce your staff:** Nothing highlights a business's personality more than getting your customers and prospective customers well acquainted with the people who will be helping them on their next visit. Include photos of employees while they are delivering a service, as well as just enjoying a nice conversation with a customer or coworker. Make sure to provide some context for why these people are a part of your team; bios are a great and often unexpected element here. Another nice touch is to include an answer to the same question with each person you introduce. "What's your favorite part about working with the [Business Name] team?" is one example.
- **Show employees performing services:** It is especially comforting for prospective customers—and/or those who have never had a specific procedure done—to know the details of what's going to happen prior to scheduling an appointment. If you've chosen to use

unique tools or technology to get the same job done, make sure to highlight your investment and tell prospective buyers why these things elevate their experience. For instance, many people have a high level of anxiety when it comes to having work done on their teeth. Dentists who offer sedation dentistry in their practices should highlight this when they talk about why it's so important to continue to focus on patient dental health. Patients can rest assured that they are well taken care of while the practice remains sensitive to whatever anxiety exists for the patient.

- **Give a tour of your business:** This is another activity that will make prospective customers more comfortable prior to entering your business. Providing a "behind the scenes" tour of your storefront or office will also get them excited about their potential future purchase experience with you.

- **Video testimonials:** Written reviews are great, but introducing a mixture of delivery methods for the same content type (in this case, reviews) empowers browsers to consume this content in the way they prefer. Your Socially Connected Consumers will likely be willing to get in front of the camera and put their face on your brand. So the next time they come in, invite them to share with the world why they love your business so much and get their 15 minutes of fame. It's easy to do; you can simply keep a camcorder behind the register or use your mobile phone to record customers giving their testimonials. You don't want them to have to come up with their own material on the fly, so create a list of questions to have readily available and ask each video reviewer a different one. Some examples might be: Why do you love our business? What keeps you coming back to [xxxx]? What's your favorite product or service and why? or How long have you been a customer? Share these video testimonials not only on your website, but also through social channels like your Facebook page.

If you haven't made your own video before, give it a try. You'll likely find that video is a fantastic way of bringing static web pages to life, and you don't need to invest a lot in tools to get started. All you need is a smart phone with a decent camera (which you or one of your employees probably has), and you can begin recording videos. A steady hand is the only additional tool you need to record your first video. You can then upload the videos from your phone to a free YouTube or Vimeo account to host. The last step is to connect your videos to the online directories and websites of your choice. Some sites, like Yelp, consider adding videos to your business profile a premium, and therefore charge for this feature. But Facebook, Merchant Circle, and many other pages (including your own website) offer this capability completely free of charge.

Formula in Action—Dr. Cynthia Brattesani

Demandforce customer Dr. Cynthia Brattesani follows a simple yet very effective formula. Her focus is to deliver a clean, professional, and informative site at www.drcynthiab.com. She focuses on using her business website as a tool to convert shoppers to buyers with repeated links to reviews and testimonials, as well as to a page on which an appointment can be scheduled (see Figure 2.7).

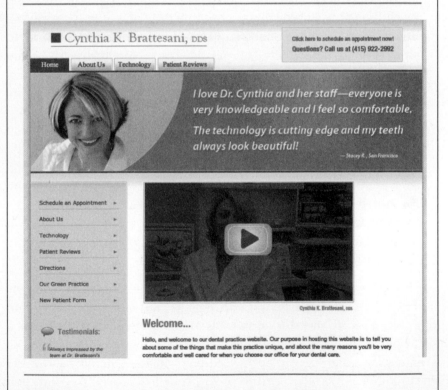

FIGURE 2.7   Dr. Cynthia Brattesani Business Website

This web page has also been designed with search in mind. The website's title includes keyword and geographical content ("San Francisco dentist"); there is enough text on each of the pages that includes keywords for the technology used, specific adjectives that describe her business practice; and the business's contact and geographical location is at the footer of every site page (see Figure 2.8).

When it comes to telling their story, the business did a great job balancing text content for search with video content to talk about the patient experience, staff, services offered, technology employed, and to provide a brief tour of the space—all in under two minutes. In addition, although images are prevalent throughout the website, there is a nice balance of text content for search engines to crawl. Something important to note is that this business's story is primarily driven by customer testimonials with secondary reinforcement through a message from the business owner on the main page of the website. They've made a conscious decision to let the customer experience, the technology employed, and the environmentally conscious practices speak for the business. This is an extremely effective way to say "I'm the best" without actually having to say it yourself.

In the Technology section of this website, the business outlines in detail some of the cutting edge technology employed by the practice, which varies from new dental equipment. As well, Dr. Brattesani leverages the technology section to let customers know the type of online communications tools the business uses to remind their patients of appointments. This is an important and often overlooked piece of the equation; educating your customers on what to expect adds a layer of comfort to what is

Dr. Cynthia Brattesani • 2001 Union St. #450 • San Francisco, CA 94123 • (415) 922-2992

FIGURE 2.8   Dr. Cynthia Brattesani Business Website Footer

(continued)

(*continued*)

frequently considered a stressful experience and can be the thing that converts customers to your business in the end.

Although the business has consciously decided to not connect their social networking profiles to their website, it is their heavy utilization of customer-generated content and video on the front page that brings the practice to life and makes this website an effective conversion tool for the business.

YOUR MAINTENANCE PLAN

Over time, your business will evolve—your logos will change, employees come and go, photos and information become outdated. It's therefore crucial for you to build simple quarterly administrative monitoring into your operational plan to address these elements without having to worry about them too much. Here are the most essential items for your maintenance plan to address:

- Important business changes need to be updated immediately. Not only do you need potential customers to find you, but search engines also use your name, address, and phone number to verify your business. You must keep information current across the entire spectrum of online directories, websites, and social sites you've decided to manage, and make necessary alterations and updates:
  - When you change or add locations
  - If you change your phone number or email address, or any other contact information
  - When you redesign your business logo
  - If your business hours are changing, including for holidays (be sure that you update your website prior to these changes to avoid confusion)
  - If you have some specials that have expired (or are about to), or when you have a new set of specials
  - If you no longer offer a service or product, or you'd like to highlight any new products or services that you're making available to your customers

As part of your quarterly monitoring on each of your profiles, your website, and your social sites, you should do the following:

- Audit your photo and video galleries and delete or add relevant content. Be sure you remove or add images based on any employee turnover.
- If you've added new products or services that you want to highlight, include the fact that you now carry these in your business description, services offered, or anywhere else that makes sense. Add additional images or videos to call attention to these newly added abilities or items. A great way to highlight these new services or products is to have a callout on your front page that says, "By popular demand, now offering. . . " or "Now offering prenatal massage after 7 P.M. for busy moms."
- If you've invested in new/better technology to deliver services to your customers, highlight this investment and talk about why you feel this is a benefit for your customers.

You can perform these maintenance tasks more than quarterly if you have the bandwidth to do so. After all, the more often you check these items for accuracy, the better off you are. Social sites are most effective when you update them regularly; one to two times per week is sufficient activity. You can download and print out a checklist here if you want to add it to your operational maintenance binder: www.wiley .com/go/smallbizhandbook.

ADVANCED ONLINE REPUTATION MANAGEMENT

Now that you've got the basics down, you can consider a few additional options for enhancing your online presence. The two discussed in this section are both paid-for services that may help potential customers find you through search engines more quickly, and may help convert browsers into shoppers more easily. The intent here is to get you acquainted with some potential options if you're looking for more. While reading this section alone won't be enough to get started with either of these services, it will give you a taste of what they offer and help you decide whether to further explore these options.

Search Engines and Paid Search

You may be wondering what the difference is between paid and unpaid, or organic, search. Paid search enables you to purchase the rights for a higher display rate for specific search terms. You are often buying something called "pay-per-click," so the overall monthly investment is often a dollar range as opposed to a fixed amount. More popular search terms cost more, but may yield better results.

Organic search is unpaid and relies solely on how optimized for search your online assets are and how relevant your content is to the search terms users are entering. The two types of search results are also displayed in different areas of the search engine's results page. While this isn't necessarily a bad thing, consumers are largely aware of the fact that businesses have paid for the added awareness. As an example, if you're searching for an electrician that services a specific zip code, Figure 2.9 shows what your Google results might look like.

Anything in the shaded box on top and everything in the right column are paid advertisements; organic search results only show up underneath

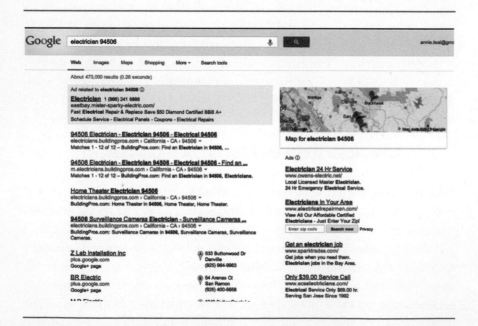

FIGURE 2.9   Google Search Results

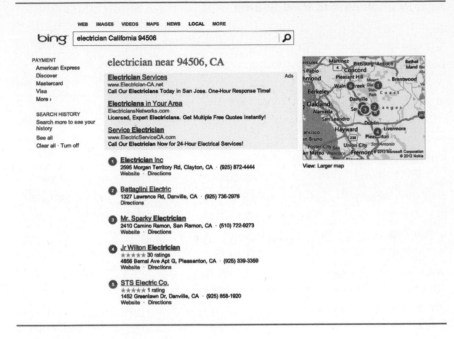

FIGURE 2.10   Bing Search Results

the pale orange ads in the left column. On Bing, the paid versus organic display results are similar (see Figure 2.10).

The challenge with paid search is that you often get what you pay for. It's a challenge for most small businesses to invest enough money to yield reasonable return, since you're usually competing with larger brands for the same real estate. However, if you're in a younger market where there may not be as much competition for the most common search terms (generally nonmetropolitan areas or suburbs to major metro areas), aren't ranking well in organic search, or have something unique to offer, it may make more sense for you to invest in paid search to significantly increase your visibility online.

Google remains the primary search engine consumers use in the United States with Bing fighting for market share. Like a few other search engines, Google sells their ad space auction style. For the buyer, this means that the highest bidder will get the best placement on the results page for relevant searches. Therefore, the amount that you pay depends on who else has bid on the same search terms and the current auction prices, so you may find yourself paying a different amount for each true click-through from your ad. To complicate things even further, Google specifically integrates a "quality score" that helps them determine how relevant the combination of your keywords, ad, and landing page (where the ad clicks go) are to the search term entered. So even if you aren't the highest bidder, you may still display higher on the search results page if your quality score indicates that your ad is more relevant to what the searcher is seeking. Figure 2.11 shows how Google describes the impact of their quality score.

Paid search isn't something that you can jump into without a strategy, especially if you are looking to maximize every marketing dollar you spend—and we hope you are! If you're thinking about investing a portion of your marketing budget in paid search, you should take some time to learn the ins and outs of the specific search engine's paid search programs you're considering, and then build a strategy around that. Many people have written entire books that serve as great introductions to paid search. At the end of this book, I've included a reference guide that lists some recommended reading for more advanced marketers.

Example

Suppose Sam is looking for a pair of striped socks. And let's say you own a website that specializes in socks. Wouldn't it be great if Sam types "striped socks" into Google search, sees your ad about striped socks, clicks your ad, and then lands on your webpage where he buys some spiffy new striped socks?

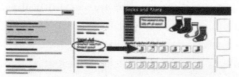

In this example, Sam searches and finds exactly what he's looking for. That's what we consider a great user experience, and that's what can earn you a high Quality Score. What's more, relevant ads tend to earn more clicks, appear in a higher position, and bring you the most success.

FIGURE 2.11   Google Quality Score
Source: http://support.google.com/adwords/answer/2454010.

Promoting with Coupons on Online Directories and Social Sites

One way to increase your conversion rate is to offer discounts for new customers who find you online. While this is an excellent way to acquire new customers faster, I will offer one word of caution. New customers who buy specifically because of a major deal you post tend to have a much lower return rate or overall lifetime value than those who were referred by an existing customer or even walked through your doors organically. Make sure you follow these best practices when deciding to use online coupons:

- Only start with one of the top three directories or social sites that your current customers typically use to find businesses like yours. For instance, if you're in a major metropolitan area in the United States, it's likely that your customers and prospective customers are using some combination of Google, Yelp, Facebook, Yahoo!, or Foursquare. In other parts of the country or world, your top list might vary. Once you identify which site is the most popular with your customers (you may have to guess when you're just starting out, which is fine for an initial test), you're on to the next step.
- Make sure you aren't posting a deal that generates negative income for your business. The unfortunate truth is that many small businesses end up losing money after their online offers are done, simply because the deal was not designed with the business's best interest in mind. Design your offer thoughtfully. Make sure you include the cost of all elements in your profit equation: the actual goods, human effort involved in delivering the service, and the "finder's fee" that's built into the site's program. If your margins are low to begin with, you may want to reconsider using online offers to attract new business. An alternate option is to offer customers non-monetary items to redeem, such as added free services with an "associated value" component like complementary upgraded services, aromatherapy for massages, service inspections, glasses of champagne, and so forth.
- The ultimate goal is to get these new customers to come back, so ensuring you are able to deliver a high level of service is of utmost importance. Stay on the lower end if you have the option to select a maximum number of deals bought, so as not to overwhelm your

staff with the heavy influx in appointment requests or traffic. Consider testing offers over time to see what creates a steady stream of traffic through this channel. For example, see how long it takes for customers to buy up 30 offers for $25 off a $50 purchase. Depending on the type of business you run, you may find that consumers *purchase* the offers quickly, but only trickle through the doors when it comes time to redeem them. Or the opposite occurs—consumers try to redeem their offer very soon after purchasing the deal, which tends to be more common. If you find that your staff isn't able to manage this influx, try keeping the volume capped but decrease the offer. You can experiment until you're able to balance both the rate of offer purchase and the rate of remittance.

It's easy to get caught up in the coupon and deal site madness to attract new customers. But you want to consider how readily these customers will actually come back and pay full price for the same service or product in the future, because this will have the greatest impact on how much these offers will improve your business.

Building a plan for your online reputation before you dive in will save you countless hours down the line, so take the time to do things right upfront and have a solid understanding of the work ahead of you. You may find that ongoing maintenance is something you can manage but initial site design is something you don't want to take on, or vice versa. You may also find that one of your employees has the skills and interest to take on these kinds of projects, which is an ideal situation for the business since you can keep things in-house and support career development for someone on your team. In the end, don't be afraid to ask for help, especially if you're under time constraints. Whatever the outcome here, the first step is to understand what you need to do, and be thoughtful about how you take on this very important piece of your business.

CHAPTER **3**

Connecting Your Offline Business with Your Online Presence

Maintaining continuity across key aspects of your offline and online worlds is necessary not only to create a consistent customer experience for online browsers but also to convert them to offline shoppers. The challenge that people often have with managing their online presence is that what is happening online is not actually a reflection of what's happening offline, and vice versa. This is usually because businesses tend to manage these two things separately, or consider one to be an afterthought, which keeps them out of sync.

In this chapter, we discuss a few things to watch out for in terms of keeping these two aspects of business connected. We also introduce some best practices that we've seen some of our customers implement in the field. But before you dive in, you must first execute the core components of your online reputation plan. Once you've covered the basics of creating, managing, and monitoring your online reputation, then you're ready to take the next step of integrating these assets into your daily offline business.

DESIGN HOLISTIC MARKETING PROMOTIONS

It can initially seem like somewhat of a burden to have to manage both your offline and online worlds. You can adjust your mindset, however, by viewing your in-store and offline marketing as an extension or a complement to your online and social marketing efforts. In reality, every promotion or marketing piece you put out into the world will likely have some representation in your core marketing channels—offline, online, and in-store. Next you'll find a simple worksheet with a promotion example that you can use for each marketing effort. This will help to ensure that you've at least *considered* how you're going to holistically leverage your core marketing channels to execute your promotion.

Goal

Generate traction around a new service the business is offering by securing 150 appointments for this service between May 1 and June 30. The cost to the business is $40; the retail cost is $95.

Promotion Details

- 20 percent off for new customers taking advantage of this service
- When an existing customer refers a new customer, the new customer gets 25 percent off the featured service, and the existing customer gets 25 percent off the featured service and then off the service of his or her choice for future referrals.

Marketing Channels

Website

- Update the Specials section on the website to reflect the offer with an anchor tag URL.
- Create a simple banner for the front page of the website that links to the Specials section.
- As testimonials and photos come in, post them on the website (this does not have to be updated as frequently as Facebook).

Social Profile(s)

- Facebook: Make an initial post on April 15 with the referral incentive offer. On May 1, publish the full promo offering with a customer testimonial. Make biweekly (or weekly, if possible) posts highlighting customers who purchase and come in for the service with their photos.
- Twitter: Post links that go directly to your Facebook updates on the same day your promotions go live.

Business Directories

- Google: Update the business description on April 30 to reflect the promotion details with a link to the Request an Appointment page on your website (or just to your website).
- Yelp: Update business description on April 30 to reflect the promotion details with a link to the Request an Appointment page on your website (or just to your website).

In-Store Experience

- Print up an 11×14 poster highlighting your promotion and affix it to the exterior window for passersby.
- Highlight an ongoing social check-in promotion in simple picture frames in the waiting area and at the register: "Get an extra $5 off any service when you show us you checked in and shared your product or service today."
- Staple-to Messaging: 2×4 coupons that you can staple to receipts. Create simple text coupons with Word or other word processer.
- Update your large service menu.
- Update your phone voicemail message.

Offline Marketing

If sending postcards, create a segment of repeat customers—those who have referred others or written great reviews in the past—and highlight the referral deal with your April 15 and May 15 postcard run.

Email Marketing

Send an email campaign on April 25 and May 25 with the promotion as the featured story. The May 25 email should include more customer testimonials and links to your Facebook page or website to learn more and request the service.

If you are a Demandforce customer, make sure to leverage your online website widgets for review publishing and appointment scheduling, and use Time.ly by Demandforce to automate your social posting to Facebook and Twitter at the best time for your followers to engage with you. In addition, maximize every email communication by segmenting your email campaigns based on when your customers last came in, how much they spent with you, or perhaps even whether they wrote positive reviews for you through your Demandforce business portal.

Looking at this worksheet, it may seem like it's going to be a lot of work to pull off this promotional campaign. But in reality, you're not looking at a huge time commitment. If you achieve your promotion goal, the return on your investment is well worth it. When you map out all of the dates and activities on a calendar, you'll see that you're dedicating at most one to two hours per week working to convert over $10,000 in incremental revenue—even *after* a 25 percent discount. You can create your own promotion worksheet, or download our template here: www.wiley.com/go/smallbizhandbook.

There's a secondary benefit of designing a holistic marketing promotion plan: Each promotion allows you to constantly test how effective each channel is with your specific customer base. No business's customer makeup is the same, so testing is necessary to understand which channels are more effective than others for converting new business and encouraging recurring business over time. For instance, you may ultimately find that social channels are extremely effective for acquiring new customers through existing customer referrals, or that always having a small new-customer promotion on your Google+ Local page creates a steady but manageable stream of new inquiries. Chapter 9 will provide more details on a few easy ways you can measure your program's success over time, which will help you continue to improve your marketing effectiveness.

The above example not only reaches across all of your core marketing channels, it also *connects* one channel to the other to maximize effectiveness. You're actively bringing your offline presence online by syndicating in-store photos and testimonials through your social channels and your website. You're also using the same promotion to ensure that no matter where online shoppers may be, they will receive the same message and convert in the same way—by requesting the service through your website. One of this deal's big bonuses is that it's structured to incentivize referral behavior, which will encourage your new customers to return. Finally, you're spreading your marketing efforts over the course of two months and providing a little bit at a time for people to respond. This allows you to leverage customer stories in the reminders you distribute across multiple channels. At the end of your holistic campaign, the service, those delivering it, and your customers become the stars who have given the promotion a nudge.

The Art of the Deal

Mastering the art of offering deals online is tricky and most businesses struggle to get it right. Having too many active promotions in too many places, and with high discounts, often brings you shoppers instead of buyers or repeat customers. It will condition casual online browsers to expect a better deal if they hold out. Not only do you burn your margins, but the notion of "suggested retail" also becomes a little bit of a running joke. Aggressively undercutting your margin to entice new customers also ends up hurting your loyal customers the most, both from the perspective of service delivery quality and in feeling compelled to remain loyal to your business. After all, why would you want to remain loyal to a business that only offered incentives to new customers?

If you publish too few or ineffective promotions throughout the year, however, your online channel becomes an ineffective conversion tool. It's a careful balancing act that will continue to evolve over the life of your business; the most important thing is to start with the right foundation so you can iterate on your promotional mix easily over time. The next chapter will provide more detail on how to design effective promotions—those that balance frequency, size, and margin, and allow you to ensure that your most loyal customers continue to feel rewarded and appreciated.

STAY CONSISTENT ACROSS CHANNELS

Because your offline and online worlds are extensions of each other, browsers and buyers alike need to experience consistency with your business when engaging with it across all the channels. If you don't inject this intentional layer of consistency into your overall marketing plan, things can quickly become misaligned.

The most critical piece of this is the look and feel of your business's brand and its brand voice. This is something you've likely already spent a great deal of time perfecting from offline and logo perspectives. In order to effectively represent your brand online, you want to invest both time and resources in a well-designed website that mirrors your offline branding. It should be the website equivalent of the experience you're trying to deliver when buyers walk through your doors. Too often, a small business hastily throws together a website merely for the purpose of *having* a website. This does more harm than good, however, because it creates a disjointed connection between your offline world and your online homestead. In addition to the core functions of your website we reviewed in Chapter 2, here are three questions you should ask yourself when designing your website to ensure that you're maintaining consistency between your offline and online worlds:

1. Does the website's look and feel represent what I feel when I walk through my business's front doors? If not, what's missing? If you're using a website building tool, you may be able to find a template design that effectively represents your business's look and feel; if not, consider investing in a designer to help you bring your offline brand feel to life online. If there's an art school in your area, try hiring a digital art student who is looking to build his or her portfolio, to keep your costs down. Most art schools have an online job board that local business owners can post to for free.
2. Does my website tell the story I want my customers to know about my business? Am I using images that effectively help tell this story? Try not to use a lot of stock photos or art on your website. Instead, use photos of your storefront and your employees to make your website experience more personal. Highlight products and services, your interior and exterior space, people, and events that showcase your business's personality and involvement with the community.
3. Do I want to have a social voice on my website that mirrors my business's Facebook page, or do I want to keep things more professional? You can do a little bit of both: Use more professional language in your website content, and simply add a Facebook plug-in that displays your Facebook post feed. This is a good option to support a "social first" feel—or actively encourage your prospective and current customers to engage with you in online

social spaces—across channels. It's perfectly fine to maintain a professional voice on your website; just make sure your social voice isn't so far off that your customers and browsers receive a disjointed experience across those channels.

Cross-channel consistency requires more than careful word choices in your promotions, website, emails, or storefront. It's also about creating an overall look and feel for the experience you are trying to deliver, and using what you've created to engage with browsers and buyers alike, no matter what platform they use to interact with your business. When online browsers *do* eventually convert to offline buyers, they'll have an added sense of familiarity with your business. Combined with the amazing service you already plan on delivering, this greatly increases your chances of creating a repeat customer.

Formula in Action: Jordan Thomas Salon & Spa

Demandforce customer Jordan Thomas Salon & Spa in Bel Air, Maryland, does a great job of integrating social and offline experiences into their overall online brand. They've focused on building a high-quality brand that is personable and that also delivers exceptional service both online and offline.

- The salon employs a simple yet effective visual tactic for creating continuity across their offline, online, and social worlds. Lindsay Smith manages the business's online accounts, and she has taken the wallpaper design from the salon and integrated it into their website and Facebook page (see Figures 3.1 through 3.3).
- Every subpage on the website uses different images. Some pages rotate through a variety of images as you stay on the page and deliver substories that complement the text. Most, if not all, of the images the site uses show the business's space and the service experience. The images highlight those who are delivering service. They have also included a salon photo album for browsers who want to see more. The business's news feed announces when new stylists are joining the team, and spreads the word about local events in which community members can get involved.
- This business takes social networking a step further than many businesses, which is a bold and effective move for them. The website's main page directly integrates their Facebook plug-in, which ensures a steady stream of new content, drives browsers to a "live" content feed with which to engage, and gives the business a little added personality on their online homestead.

FIGURE 3.1   Business Logo and In-Store Wall

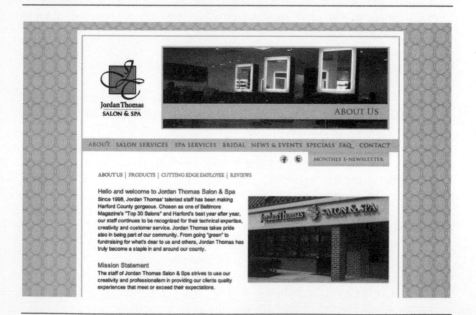

FIGURE 3.2   Website Featuring In-Store Wallpaper Design

FIGURE 3.3   Facebook Page

FIGURE 3.4   Facebook Feed Shown on Website

(See Figure 3.4.) They've made the conscious decision to keep their voice more social here, and with almost 1,600 followers and 1,200 check-ins, it's a strategy that's proving extremely effective.

ENABLE YOUR STAFF TO DELIVER
YOUR PREFERRED EXPERIENCE

You've heard it many times before, because it's the truth: Happy customers start with happy employees. And happy employees are the ones who are prepared to do their jobs well and deliver the "experience expectations" you've set via your online and offline marketing efforts. Employees are also likely to encourage add-on services, thereby increasing average revenue per customer for your business.

You want to ensure you are giving your employees the best possible chance to deliver the experience you want customers to have. To that end, you want to build a set of standard operating procedures into your marketing plan, with specific guidelines on communication, positioning, experience delivery, and product or service upselling, if relevant. Create an overview information sheet for every promotion that includes the following information, and share that document with your employees a few weeks before the promotion is scheduled to go live:

- A copy of the creative (or promotional piece—coupon, image, etc.)
- Promotional messaging and details
- Remittance and expiration information
- Channels you're using to deliver this message, and anything potentially unique about the messaging through these specific channels
- Instructions on how to record the promotion in your POS system for bookkeeping purposes and to measure results
- Details on any internal promotion you have to drive activity from within the business

After distributing the information sheet, follow up with a quick meeting to review the promotion's details. Use this gathering as an opportunity to bring your employees into the fold of designing and executing great marketing plans for your business. You might be surprised at how much your team will have to contribute, and how much they appreciate being a part of the creative process.

If you don't have to follow specific franchise marketing guidelines, you and your team can decide on the most effective ways to pitch the promotion through all channels, including in-store. Review any in-store collateral you'll be using throughout the space and work with your employees to agree on where you'll place signage, samples, and videos, and when you'll do so. Ask your team for ideas on what other products or services would be great to merchandise along with the promotional items to get their support in making the promotion successful. The more you encourage your employees to share their ideas, the more involved they'll become, and the more successful your promotion will be.

You want to welcome as much active participation as you can from those involved in the planning and program execution design processes. This creates an environment of learning and collaboration that has the added benefit of enhancing employee satisfaction and getting your team even more invested in the program's success. It provides an often unexpected outlet for your employees to get their creative juices flowing. It also lets them learn about the behind-the-scenes aspects of the business that they may not have access to working elsewhere, which can potentially increase overall employee retention and value. If you haven't tested this practice at your business before, try it out just once and see what happens. You may be surprisingly pleased with the results on all fronts.

DELIVER CONSISTENCY THROUGH YOUR SOCIAL VOICE

You'll have to pay special attention to how you market your ongoing communications regarding your promotions for each specific social channel. Remember, your social style should reflect your offline experience, and vice versa. As discussed previously, some businesses prefer to maintain a more professional tone through their social channels, something that often transcends well when communicating the logistics behind special online offers. Other businesses prefer to lighten their tone through social channels to use this as an opportunity to inject some spice into their business. Following are examples of different styles two businesses use to post promotions on their Facebook pages:

- Dave's Ultimate Automotive in greater Austin, Texas, uses a fun and engaging image to celebrate National Car Care Month. His tone is more relaxed and he injects some fun with the American colloquialism *TLC* (see Figure 3.5).

FIGURE 3.5   Dave's Ultimate Automotive Facebook Promotion

- AvantGard Spa in San Carlos, California, takes a more professional tone with their last minute offer (shown in Figure 3.6). It delivers the message cleanly without any extra fuss, which has proven to be extremely effective for their target audience.

Because it's likely that social posting will be a shared responsibility at the business, carefully communicate the tone you want employees to use on Facebook, Twitter, Pinterest, and other social sites you use. Setting expectations on tonality, frequency, and response time from the very start will help you create empowered employees who feel confident that they have the right tools to successfully execute on your vision.

Regardless of whether you decide to make your business's social tone more fun or more professional, remember that nothing is set in stone. It's okay to evolve over time. You might find that your initial decision was appropriate in the beginning, but you've gradually found that customers and fans who engage with you through your social channels prefer something a little different. It's completely fine—and actually, very

FIGURE 3.6   AvantGard Spa Facebook Promotion

wise—to adapt your voice to be more in line with that of your followers. As long as you keep your listening skills sharp, you and your team will have no trouble reading your community and tweaking your social voice to keep customers satisfied.

Your tactics might also depend on how mature your business's marketing program is. You may find that simply starting with the first piece—leveraging a holistic marketing plan with each promotion—is as far as you can get right now. That is a perfectly acceptable place for many newer businesses to start. Soon enough you'll be able to test channel effectiveness and determine where you should be spending your energy.

Maintaining consistency across all of your marketing channels, including the in-store experience, is critical to delivering a winning customer experience. The businesses that connect their offline and online worlds most effectively tend to think of program design and execution from a holistic point of view. They consider the implications across all relevant marketing channels from the beginning, and express a consistent feel using tools like language, brand, and visual imagery. In addition, these businesses pay special attention to the unique nature of communicating through their social channels, and aren't afraid to evolve their strategies over time.

No matter how your online shoppers interact with your business, they'll feel that sense of consistency when they convert to offline buyers who walk through your doors. All of the best practices discussed here will help you develop the right environment for converting browsers to customers. However, you still need the right *types* of offers to maximize your online marketing channels. In Chapter 4, we dive into designing online offers that convert shoppers to *buyers*.

CHAPTER **4**

Online Offers That Convert into Lasting Business

The tricky thing about offering deals to acquire new customers is that much of the "deal shopper" segment has already been conditioned to keep looking for *new* bargains for similar services and products. This makes customer loyalty even more difficult to maintain when targeting this segment. Companies who successfully leverage offers and promotional campaigns to drive business are continually working to balance new customers against existing ones, as well as striving to consistently deliver exceptional service. We'll spend some time talking about deal-driven new customer acquisition here; however, we'll dedicate most of the conversation to discussing offers that provide you with a greater chance of retaining customers *after* the deals are over. But before we get into the details of designing deals specific to new customer acquisition or achieving your retention targets, let's first take the time to look at the anatomy of a deal.

ANATOMY OF A DEAL

Every deal, whether it's delivered through online or offline channels, is comprised of four basic components that we'll break down in detail. No matter what time of year, how big or small the deal, what kind of company you are, or what medium you use to inform others about your promotion, every single offer must provide the following the four Ws to prospective customers: who, what, why, and when.

Follow this simple formula every time, and at a minimum you will publish offers that deliver all of the necessary information for online browsers to make intelligent decisions about whether they want to work with your business. Designing an offer that misses in one of these areas is an expensive marketing error to make. You will often be forced to deliver on an experience that closes the gap between customer expectations (that are rooted in assumption due to lack of information) and your own uncommunicated assumptions about the same offer.

Who: Know Who You're Trying to Convert

Every time you decide to publish a promotion, you need to consider who you are targeting to redeem that offer. Once you know who you are trying to convert, and why you believe this is a great group to go after, the details come into focus much more quickly. This section will discuss the potential target segments you might consider as well as decisions your segmentation choice impacts.

The most basic customer segments to start with are new customers versus repeat customers, without additional distinctions of geographic, demographic, or behavioral segmentation. Depending on where your business lies in terms of market maturity, you may find that you've acquired a strong enough customer base and want to build loyalty. Perhaps you've found that customers on average visit your business five times in a year and then somehow drop off; therefore, you need to steadily continue to obtain new customers to backfill the loss in revenue with new customer acquisition. Maybe your business is on the newer side with a small but loyal following and you want to maximize the referral channel to slowly bring on high-quality customers. Every business has different needs for targeting; understanding your *who* in this instance is critical to your marketing campaign's success.

Let's say that you do have a newer business and haven't been able to confidently define your current customer base and which segments respond to your marketing programs. In this case, you may initially decide to segment more generically, and limit the total number of offers that customers can redeem. This combination serves the primary purpose of ensuring that you can test for acceptable redemption rate and manage whatever business converts from your promotion. Initially, you may not see a substantial return on your early promotions, but starting small is the best way to test your effectiveness, market interest, and ability to simultaneously manage your bandwidth to deliver on the best possible experience for your entire customer base. And because every company's customer base has its own unique makeup, the success of your initial promotions (or lack thereof) will provide the feedback and lessons you'll need to determine how to best balance these three over time.

There are a million different ways to go in terms of identifying the right target segment. Depending on how much information you have about your customers and how well you've organized that information, you have the opportunity to be very specific about how you target your customer offers. You'll likely be able to design more sophisticated promotions models as a result. Here are some common segmentation types leveraged by Demandforce customers:

Behavioral

- Time since last visit or purchase
- Products purchased
- Amount spent
- Services performed
- Average review rating
- Customers who would recommend
- Future appointment or visit scheduled
- Connected to the business through social channels

Demographic

- Age
- Service provider
- Gender
- Insurance type
- Communication preference type
- Birthday or anniversary

If you have enough information on customer behavior, it's ideal to initially focus your segmentation efforts there. Targeting the conversation based on customer behavior allows you to be very specific about what you are promoting and use past behavior to help you decide on what kind of discount to offer—not too much and not too little. Demographic driven segmentation can also be an extremely effective segmentation model. For example, someone in cosmetic medicine practice may know that females between the ages of 35 and 55 have the highest purchase history for Botox treatments; they could use this information, combined with their customer demographic information, to market these treatments.

You can also mix demographic and behavioral segmentation, such as offering a 15 percent discount on baby clothing and accessories to females between the ages of 22 and 45 who have purchased a crib or other nursery furniture in the past six months. In this way, you really start to customize your offerings.

Again, the more information you've collected upfront about your customers, the better prepared you will be to build an effectively segmented marketing campaign. If you don't have the types of information noted above, keep your offers more general until you know what will stick (and with whom). Go back to the drawing board and identify ways you can incorporate data collection into the purchase experience (see the customer survey sample in Chapter 1 as an example).

It's important to note that several factors are relevant to how your target segments respond to your offer, including the channels you use for advertising, your timing, and the types of messages you convey. Depending on your target, you may decide that it's more effective to only use social media or to only send an email campaign to a specific segmentation within your email database. If you're testing for general response, you may choose a more holistic marketing campaign and leverage all the available marketing channels. If you aren't sure what the right combination is initially, don't be afraid to test different permutations and see which combination generates the return you're seeking. This is something you will determine in part through the *what*, which we will discuss next.

Your Best Customers Come from Referrals

Businesses are frequently so busy focusing their energy on acquiring new customers and delivering a consistent experience to their customer base that they often neglect their most valuable customer segment: active referrers. Though this might be just a small percentage of your customer segment, it's critical that you have at least a basic program in place to support and encourage their activity.

The benefit of acquiring a new customer through your referral channel is that these customers already have a vested interest in your success; it's been channeled through the referrer. They will therefore be more likely to work with you if they encounter a problem during their purchase experience, and may also be more apt to tell others about their (hopefully positive) experiences. We'll further discuss the details of designing a customer rewards program in

Chapter 8. In the meantime, consider the following five initial tips for designing offers that continue to nurture your most valuable customers:

1. **Reward the referrer *and* the referee.** This should be an easy modification if you already have a new customer acquisition deal in place. Even if you don't have a formal offer that rewards the existing customer for bringing in new business, find a way to say thank you. Put a note on that person's account to give them a little something the next time they come in. The gift could be as small as a coupon for their next purchase, a Starbucks gift card, or gift card for a future service.

2. **Provide an incentive to get the referred customer back a second time as a part of the referral program.** It's the same as when you're designing deal site promotions or any other new customer acquisition program: building in a strategy that incentivizes that new customer to return a second time provides you with additional leeway and a captive audience. New customer acquisition through your referral channel is no exception to this rule.

3. **Reward customers with retail products instead of services offered to increase perceived value.** If you have a retail component to your business, make sure you find ways to leverage this channel. Offering retail items is a great way to increase perceived value due to the built-in mark up from cost. For example, at a salon, the retail price of a bottle of shampoo may be $22, but the wholesale price is half that at $11. Including the bottle of shampoo or any other product with a 100 percent markup significantly increases the value of the service delivered to the customer without impacting your bottom line.

4. **Encourage gift card purchases into your customer base as a key driver of referral business.** This is a great way to broaden the scope of your actively referring customer base. Gift cards are an easy and thoughtful way of giving for those who may not necessarily know exactly what to get for a specific occasion or person. For those customers who are evangelists for your business in the offline or online world, gift cards are also an easy way for them to introduce their friends and family to a business they love. In addition, if you don't have a solid handle on precisely *which* customers are referring business to you, putting an aggressive gift card promotion out there is a great first step. For tracking purposes, you can append the gift cards with some internal coding; if you're printing them out, simply use a different color for easy coding.

5. **Don't discount the power of handing out some business cards to your favorite customers.** Asking for the referral is often the most difficult part of building a referral program; however, you need to educate your customers on how they can help support your business, especially in the beginning. Even if you don't establish a formal referral program, you can use business cards as an easy conversation starter. Simply hand the customer three business cards at the point of sale and say, "I'd really appreciate it if you could let a few friends know about the great service you received today."

Of course, your active referrers are most likely sending new customers your way just because they love your business. It's very possible that they don't expect or even want incentives for referring. So before you spend the time designing a referral program based on monetary reward, test out how willing your customers are to simply help spread the word.

What: Define the Scope of Your Offer

When identifying your offer's *what*, start by first understanding how much additional business you're looking for. You can characterize it either as time ("I have 10 one-hour appointment slots I would like to fill per week"), dollar amount ("I would like to add an incremental $700 revenue in retail items sold per week"), or even customer mix ("I would like to add 25 new customers in this age demographic, who use social media, or who were referred by current clients").

If you've initially targeted your opportunity by customer mix or are limiting your offer redemption amount, then it should be fairly easy to determine your segmentation rules. If you're targeting by anything else and not setting an upper limit for redemptions, then you'll want to filter your total market opportunity until you reach an initially aggressive 5 to 7 percent conversion. This will give you a buffer and keep you from being overwhelmed by the additional business.

Depending on your average ticket or purchase size, you should vary the language you use to publish your offer in order to drive the highest conversion and redemption rate. For example, businesses that bill under $100 per ticket on average should describe their discounts as a dollar amount off a minimum purchase (e.g., $10 off a $50 purchase, or simply $10 off your next purchase when you have a relatively predictable average purchase price). Those that bill over $100 per ticket should focus their language on a percent off total amount. Companies often append this kind of offer to specific products, retail items, or for labor, as well as potentially with a max discount value. For example, saying "10 percent off labor for services over $149 (max $75 value)" is a common way for businesses to both publish an attractive offer and limit liability at the upper limit for the higher ticket services.

If you don't know your average ticket or purchase amount, you should review an off-season month's books and create a high level estimate by dividing total revenue by the number of purchase visits. If you still don't have a good sense of average ticket or purchase price, consider testing both models that amount to the same minimum value and identifying which offer type creates the highest number of returns for your business.

Let's go into some detail about four specific kinds of offers to which you want to pay special attention throughout the life of your business.

Offers That Drive Repeat Business Oftentimes, a nudge is all it takes to encourage existing customers to come back to you when you're making an effort to prompt repeat business. This segment of your customer base already knows that they're going to receive excellent service from you; therefore, you don't necessarily have to heavily discount your product or service to convince them to return. Here are some offers we've seen convert well among the Demandforce customer base to give you an idea of what other businesses in your industry are doing to drive recurring business:

Industry	Offer
Accounting	• Complimentary three-year audit with federal and state tax preparation
Automotive body shops	• Fix up those car dings—$49 special • 10 percent off parts and labor
Automotive dealership	• 10 percent off OEM accessories • Complimentary car wash • Complimentary shuttle
Automotive repair	• Free wiper blades with your service over $49 • Complimentary 29-point inspection • Complimentary car wash with tune-up • $7 off your next oil change or $10 off any service over $50
Chiropractic	• Buy five adjustments, get one free • We haven't seen you in a while, complimentary reevaluation • Complimentary X-rays for new or referred patients • End of year insurance reminder

(*continued*)

Industry	Offer
Cosmetic medicine	• 10 percent off Botox package • Three photofacials for $179
Dental	• 10 or 15 percent off teeth whitening • Complimentary X-rays with your first cleaning • End of year insurance reminder
Dermatology	• 20 percent off selected skincare lines • $359 five-session skin-spot laser removal
Gardening and landscaping	• 20 percent off every other visit with biweekly plan • Get your garden ready for spring—15 percent off mulching and fertilization
HVAC	• $59 duct cleaning • $39 furnace tuning • $39 "green your house" consultation and testing
Optometry	• 15 percent off your annual supply of contact lenses • Free eyeglass cleaning kit with your visit • Buy one pair of glasses, get 20/30/40 percent off the second pair • End of year insurance reminder
Plumbing	• $15 off for new customers • Grout and sealant special: $89 to reseal your kitchen and bath
Retail	• $10 off $49 purchase • 10 percent off your next visit • Free accessory wall pick of your choice with $50 purchase
Salon	• $49 hair extensions • $29 Keratin treatments with cut and style • $129 cut, color, and shoulder massage

Industry	Offer
Spa	• Complimentary express manicure with $99 service • Get upgraded to the deluxe facial when you buy a package of three signature facials • 15 percent off gift certificates $100 or over
Veterinary	• $15 off this and your next visit • Half off microchipping with your check-up • 10 percent off flea- and tick-control products
Wealth management	• Complimentary annual planning session

The offers noted above fall into one of three categories:

1. The amount discounted is not so aggressive that your business experiences a loss in revenue.
2. The discounted offer is redeemed as an add-on to another full-priced product or service.
3. The offer is a complimentary service that is intended to add value to an existing full-priced service.

Because these offers are meant to nudge your existing customers and convert those who were considering purchasing at some recent point in time, your goal is to offer *enough* to tilt the purchase decision in your favor. You also want a steady, manageable stream of business as opposed to surges that create large influxes in your ability to deliver on quality. We recommend presenting periodic offers, such as once every one or two months, through inexpensive channels like email marketing to keep your brand at the top of people's minds and tactfully prod your existing customers to come back.

The "No Discount" Offer Of course, not every business feels the need to or even *wants* to publish discounted offers to get customers through the door. You may well find, once you do some testing within your own customer base, one of a few unexpected outcomes listed below that leads you to the same conclusion:

• The types of customers you are attracting from publishing these offers do not align well with the *type of business* you want to be. New customer acquisition through a heavy dose of promotions frequently results in higher overall churn. Therefore, your role as a small business owner is to continue to put more effort into generating *new* business, since you cannot provide the same level of discounts to these new customers. The long-term ramifications include how effective relationship building will be with this customer segment, and this impacts elements like overall effectiveness via social channels, long-term community engagement, and your ability to increase average revenue per customer over time.

- The types of customers you are attracting do not align well with the *customer segments* you are interested in. Especially for last-minute shoppers, online deals can be a lifesaver and enormous source of gratification. If a reasonable percentage of your customer base is comprised of these last-minute-deal shoppers, then you might find that your calendar frequently has open slots that fill up last minute or that you have a significant amount of regular revenue from sale-driven purchases. This can be a high source of stress for business owners and managers. Customer loyalty and retention is also a valid concern here.

- Your business is not able to effectively sustain the high surge of traffic driven by promotions, and as a result, you experience a decline in your public review ratings. This is like a double-edged sword—you want the business, but you don't want it like this. This is sometimes referred to as the *Groupon effect*, and it's the topic of a 2012 study by Yale University researcher Georgios Zervas and a team of peers who made the connection between Groupon deals and an immediate decline in Yelp ratings. Zervas also cited a compelling quote in a blog post[1] discussing his team's findings: "Groupon, in a recent NPR program[2] discussing our work, commented: 'It's been documented that anytime an influx of customers visits a business their online reviews tend to see a decrease in quality. This effect holds true for online as well as traditional advertising such as print, broadcast, radio.'" Although you can establish some controls to limit your exposure to unmanageable surges in volume, many businesses often feel compelled to make the

---

[1]"The Groupon Effect on Yelp Ratings," http://mybiasedcoin.blogspot.com/2012/03/groupon-effect-on-yelp-ratings-guest.html.
[2]"For Some Businesses, Daily Deals Have a Dark Side," www.npr.org/2012/07/06/156333505/for-some-businesses-daily-deals-have-a-dark-side.

most of the exposure and set their limits higher than they can manage. Of course, a negative impact ensues when you're not able to offer preferred scheduling. Your existing customers see diminished service, and you aren't able to keep up with demand and deliver the level of service you have in the past.

With the proliferation of daily deal sites (nearly 1,800 existed as of 2011 alone,[3] but over 700 of them also folded by the time 2011 was over),[4] it's fairly likely that your business has been approached by one of these companies in the past year. And you've probably dabbled with the idea of publishing this kind of deal. You may actually experience more than one or even all three of these outcomes throughout the life of your business. That said, if you didn't have a great experience the first time, don't let that one bad experience prevent you from tweaking how you approach offers through deal sites and trying again. It's very possible that altering your strategy or making your offer a little more conservative will generate the kinds of results you're looking for without completely overwhelming your business.

Deep Discounts and Deal Sites for New Customer Acquisition Many small businesses these days feel like they need to go gangbusters on new customer deals just to get online shoppers' attention and traffic. If you're targeting this segment, then yes, you'll probably need to offer a deep enough discount to compete with other businesses in your area that are honing in on the same customers. Following are some tips on how you can more effectively leverage deal sites and drive new business, without breaking the bank:

- **Be *selective* about who you work with.** Deal sites come in a variety of flavors, and with an even greater variety of terms. Some are more favorable toward small businesses than others. Don't automatically assume you need to work with Groupon or LivingSocial because they're the two biggest players. There are probably hundreds of deal

---

[3]Lauren Cannon, "Overcoming the Groupon Effect," www.youngentrepreneur.com/startingup/startup-business-ideas/overcoming-the-groupon-effect-how-to-sell-merchants-on-your-start-up-deal-site/.
[4]"Is the Deal Finally Done?" www.retailprophet.com/blog/advertising/is-the-deal-finally-done/.

sites that service your geographical region, and they are not only potentially more niche to your product or service but also more willing to negotiate with you. Ask to take a look at analytics on the types of offers that have converted successfully with their user install base over the past 30 to 60 days, as well as sales in your geographic market and service type for the past few quarters. Don't just take the sales rep's word when he or she discusses conversion rates in your market—someone who just bought a massage three days ago likely isn't going to buy another massage deal right away. In addition, buyers often follow cyclical patterns when making online purchases. You have to analyze this trend data over time to determine how successful you might be with converting new customers through this channel.

- **Assess your risk *before* you sign on.** Deal sites remain in business because they can be extremely lucrative. . . for the deal site. Make sure you review the terms of several deal sites *in detail* to get a firm grasp on what exactly you're signing up for. Here are some questions to ask if you can't find answers in the terms sheet:
  - What is the payout schedule?
  - Is the deal site paying for the credit card processing fees?
  - Are you penalized for offering add-ons?
  - Can I also sell through another deal site (either at the same time or after this deal is over)?
  - What happens if I need to back out or close the deal early?
  - Do I have ownership of my customer data?
  - Will you ever share my personal contact information?
  - Can I amend the "fine print" if I need to once it's been published?
  - What happens if the deal site makes an error?
  - When is revenue realized from a taxation and reporting standpoint?

  Remember, it is your responsibility to protect your own rights and those of your business. Read the terms of your business agreement in full before you sign on the dotted line.

- **Create an offer that meets *your company's* needs, not the needs of the deal site.** Deal sites are often seeking a specific type of offering for their customer base—be it a particular service, product, discount offered, price point, or deal volume. You may therefore feel that certain sites try to force your business into offering one of a specific set of templated deals, since that's what they believe sells.

They might also have a minimum percent discount off retail pricing in order to qualify for publication. If you've run the numbers and cannot say with confidence that publishing a deal with this site will generate both acceptable levels of revenue and volumes your business can effectively manage, then you might want to consider working with another company that will support your goals.

- **Don't bite off more than you can chew.** The best way of ensuring you are creating a solution instead of a problem is by hedging your bets. The easiest way to do this is to cap the upper limit of how many deals you can sell. Another option is to increase the volume and lower the discounted amount to reduce the number of deep-discount shoppers who purchase your deal. By separating the thriftiest shoppers at the beginning, you put yourself in a better position to have customers return a second and third time with a mix of your retail pricing model and other less aggressive incentives. Most importantly, make sure you clearly understand the levels of service your current employees can deliver, as well as what kinds of staffing flexibility you have if you find yourself needing extra help. Even with all the trend data in the world, you never know when your deal on one of these sites is going to take off.

- **Create a plan to get those new customers back again.** On average, 80 percent of the people who purchase your deal will be customers you've never seen before. In addition, businesses that regularly use these sites (i.e., they run seven or more deals) are able to convert an average of one-third of these customers into repeat buyers.[5] This customer segment is used to surfing the web and getting deal after deal after deal. Therefore, you need to design follow-up packages that not only support the buyer's desire to feel like he or she is getting great value from your business, but that also speak to the more relationship-driven side of supporting small companies. Another way to encourage return business is by allowing both new and existing customers to purchase your deal site offer, or by allowing new customers to purchase the same offer multiple times for their

---

[5]Utpal M. Dholakia, "How Businesses Fare with Daily Deals as They Gain Experience: A Multi-Time Period Study of Daily Deal Performance," June 25, 2012. Available at SSRN: http://ssrn.com/abstract=2091655 or http://dx.doi.org/10.2139/ssrn.2091655.

personal use. While you do decrease your overall margin across the entire customer base, there are benefits to this strategy:

- Existing customers don't feel like they need to deal shop other businesses in order to receive the same discount levels as new customers.
- By enabling new customers to purchase multiples, you are already building in the repeat visit(s) and are giving yourself the extra time to build rapport and customer loyalty.

The desired outcome for working with deal sites is ultimately to make sure that whatever deal gets published has a positive impact on the business, so take all the precautionary measures necessary to ensure that you'll be able to deliver.

TIP—Be Careful of the First Visit Curse

Doing an amazing job during the first visit may get the customer to come back a second time. However, it's even more important to deliver the same or higher quality of experience with *each subsequent visit*. Customers are often paying more in ensuing visits, so you'll want to incorporate ways to make them feel extra special and make it your primary objective to deliver an exceptional experience that gets the customer to return again. Service-based business owners will almost always tell you that the ultimate goal during the checkout process is to confirm the next appointment. A retailer's goal is to make the customers feel like they connected with the business and compel them to want to spend time there.

If the second visit is likely to occur awhile after the first, try injecting periodic reminders about your business that keep the positive experience alive. If you were able to collect the customer's email address, send a thank you note that invites them to join you on Facebook to keep in touch. You might even include a request to write a public review. If you prefer an offline touch, mail a handwritten note and include a coupon to "bring a friend" next time. Take the opportunity to remind these customers what an incredible first experience they had so that it'll be worth every penny to them when it's time to pay again.

There are dozens of ways to design the scope of an offer well. As long as you are able to say with confidence that you're willing to test for results and you've done your due diligence in verifying that your offer doesn't negatively affect your business, then you are in a great position to start finding the right mix of the 4 Ws for your business.

Why: Provide a Compelling Reason to Buy. . .

There are two *whys* you need to answer for the consumer: "Why buy from *you*?" and "Why buy *today*?"

Designing a compelling *why* statement is a mix of art and science, and we'll spend some time talking about both throughout this section. The response to the first question typically doesn't change much over time because the answer is often rooted in why you went into business in the first place. By now, you've hopefully created a foundation with your online presence that effectively tells your business's story in a compelling way. This will serve the purpose of delivering your *why* message. If this is still on your to-do list, I recommend you revisit Chapter 2, download your checklist, and get to work. You need a basic foundation for prospective customers to learn about you and come to their own conclusions as to why they should support your business. Otherwise, your overall return on online efforts will be significantly lower.

Conversely, your messaging strategy around "Why buy today?" depends primarily on your target audience and may also vary based on the specific offer you're publishing. That is, if you're trying to acquire new customers, you don't have the luxury of them knowing what a great experience you deliver. Therefore with potential customers, you may need to adjust your language to be more aggressive on the offer and be more deliberate with using time-sensitive promotions. On the other hand, you may be able to leverage a more personal tone with existing customers—one that helps them recall what great experiences their prior visits were.

As far as the deal itself goes, there are two basic pieces to the puzzle for designing a great promotion to address why customers should buy *today*: pictures and words.

Visual Elements First, you absolutely do *not* have to go out and hire a designer to create fantastic promotional imagery for every offer. The reason for tying visuals to an offer is to help set a context for the offer's purpose. It's also intended to catch the prospective customers' eyes and draw their attention to where you want them to focus, which is of course the call to action (redeem now, click here, buy online, request an appointment, etc.). Use of images depends on the scope of your promotion as well as the channel you use to deliver the message; not every offer warrants an image. In some cases, the offer itself might be enough to compel customers to click, call, or drive over to your business. If you do decide to connect an image to the offer, consider ways to make this imagery personal. For instance, one of Demandforce's customers recently decided to run a new customer referral campaign that included a TV giveaway drawing at the end of a one-month period. The picture they used in the email marketing campaign, on the website, and on their Facebook page was of the employees holding up the TV in a box, smiling, and waving to readers inviting them to join in on the promotion.

This formula—mixing the people with the product and the experience—is a great combination for small businesses. Whereas people generally expect big brands to feature flashy ad spots and highly stylized designs, the public largely embraces small businesses when they focus heavily on putting the people and experiences before the brand. So take advantage of the fact that you are a small business, a brand of your own, and an active part of your community. Don't be afraid to show that off in every aspect of your work, including promotions.

Another effective visual element that can be used in your offers is a button that indicates that your prospective customers can and should act right now. A frequent call to action for service-based business offers is to "request an appointment" or "request a quote." Especially through the email channel and on websites, placing the call-to-action button below the offer usually provides enough imagery to get your message across.

The simplistic nature of keeping the imagery focused on a single call to action can be an appealing option for many small business owners. You benefit on a number of fronts—namely, by keeping design costs minimal by reusing the same easy-to-understand visual elements in one campaign after another. What's even more important, though, is the fact that as your customers continue to receive offers from you through the various marketing channels, they are able to visually sense the similarities over time. They don't have to think about what they need to do in order to redeem your offer.

Making it easy for customers to redeem offers is certainly a part of answering the "Why buy today?" question, and it's something you can't ignore. If you are asking people to print something out, then call for an appointment, *then* provide some information online in advance of the appointment, your redemption rate will significantly drop. For every additional step potential customers have to take, and every piece of unnecessary information that they have to provide, your conversion rate sees double-digit percentage drops.

The lesson here is to keep things as simple as possible at all times. Imagery is important, but don't let the visuals you incorporate into your marketing campaign outshine the offer itself. Consider leveraging images as a conversion tool and call to action in your campaign instead of a marketing tool. Keep in mind that the more you ask of your prospects across the board, the harder it will be to get them to redeem the offer and walk through your doors.

Language of the Sale The words you choose to convey your message about why customers should buy today are critical. They give you the opportunity to draw your prospective customers in, help them understand what's most important to you and your business, or simply create a sense of urgency if that's what you're looking to do. Thanks to the added visibility of online directories, customer reviews, and syndicated offers in today's Internet economy, your business must compete with other local businesses within a significantly larger geographic radius.

There's a positive element to this, of course: your business has the opportunity to capture customers within that same much larger pool. And because you're starting with a bigger selection, it's crucial to use the appropriate tools to stand out to the *right* potential customers. Depending on how you position yourself in the marketplace, you could very well draw the kinds of customers you *don't* want—deep-discount seekers, overly unreasonable customers, unreliable customers, or those who have a tendency not to pay. No matter how badly you want the new business, you need to consider the ramifications these kinds of customers have on your business. You certainly don't want them to impede your ability to take proper care of those already walking through your door, or negatively impact your return rate or lifetime value in the longer term. In the end, it may be better to be a little conservative rather than very sorry when offering deep discount promotions to new customers in the small business space.

Now that you've given some thought to how you want to position yourself in the marketplace and how your promotions impact the types of customers you'll get, it's time to start building your *why* story.

When it comes to selecting the right words and phrases to tell your story, you'll want to adjust your positioning on why customers should buy today based on the scope of your selected offer. Here are some tips on how to tell your *why* story effectively with words:

- **Be factual.** Feel free to take creative liberty with adjectives and color, but never overexaggerate to the point that quality, quantity, value, or your business's integrity come into question once a prospect becomes a buyer. Using numbers is often an effective way to communicate value with a bang—for instance, "94 percent of customers saw an immediate difference after the first session."

- **Leverage someone else's reputation.** If a magazine has recently highlighted this product or service, use that to your advantage and word your offer around this. Keep in mind that you may need to deal with copyright issues when repurposing material from other sources; however, it should be fairly easy to link to the magazine's site. Frequently used phrases here are "As seen in *Lucky* magazine and on Reese Whitherspoon" or "Rated a Best Buy by *Consumer Reports*."

- **Use existing customer recommendations and testimonials.** If you have a recent customer review that emphasizes how amazing this product or service is, turn that recommendation into a referral engine by pitching your offer as "customer approved" and share the customer's story. You can go several directions here: including a customer video testimonial, before and after photos, a quotation from the customer's review. . . . All are effective ways to draw new business from your current fans.

- **Be as brief as possible.** The fewer words you can use to convey your message, the better off you are. Your marketing campaign needs to be compelling enough to generate that click, call, or whatever action you're seeking (oftentimes, this is a mix). Try to get your pitch down to one sentence and under 10 words. Depending on the channel (such as with AdWords), you may even have as few as 25 characters in your heading to pitch your offer.

- **Highlight association tie-ins if there are any.** Small businesses frequently develop promotions around events sponsored by well-known brands, associations, and institutions. For instance, many auto shops take advantage of Car Care's National Car Care Month in April and October. They drive heavy volumes of activity by reminding their customers to get their checkups and prepare for summer and winter vehicle usage. Another more recent and popular nationwide event, regardless of your industry or specialization, is Small Business Saturday, which is the Saturday after Thanksgiving each year.

- **Use words that create a sense of urgency.** Your offers—*especially* those last minute ones to fill open calendar slots or help you close the month stronger—need the right words to help create a sense of urgency. Instead of just *why*, you're trying to answer the question "Why *right now*?" Use words and phrases like "limited time," "first 10," "one time offer," "book today and receive a bonus," "final sale," "final inventory," or "one day sale." Action phrases that evoke a potential sense of loss for *not* taking advantage of the offer are a great way to increase immediate conversion. Another way to create a sense of urgency is to combine this tactic with channels that are effective for delivering the message. For instance, social media is a very effective method of promoting last minute deals due to the nature of interaction and expectations that are already built into the platform.

When you marry the right visual elements with verbiage that drives your message home and effectively answers the "why" questions for your prospective customers, you create a powerful combination that can deliver impressive results for your business. However, that "perfect marriage" is not set in stone; it depends in large part on the offer itself. It takes time to figure out how your customer base will respond to the different types of stories you tell through the various channels you use to publish offers, so don't be afraid to test and measure for results. Chapter 9 will provide further details on effective testing strategies that small businesses can easily put to work to help measure marketing success over time.

When: Timing Is (Pretty) Important

In the online marketing world, it's crucial to consider the day and time you publish and communicate your offer—especially in terms of the channel you're using. If, for instance, you're emailing an offer, you want to avoid sending your marketing campaign too early in the day because your email will end up in prospective customer's inboxes with dozens of other marketing offers. Figure 4.1 shows an inbox on a Saturday morning, which is typically one of the lowest-volume days for email marketing.

Bloomingdale's	Online & In Store--Home Sale and HOT - Home Sale Ends Tomorrow! Having problems viewing this email? Click here. Shop	5:51 am
Coach by Invitation	Don't Miss Out, Enjoy 25% Off Now! - Final days to enjoy 25% off your entire purchase! Use it now and enjoy FREE SHIPPIN	5:26 am
Bloomspot	Near You: $35 Cut, $145 Brazilian Blowout (Union Sq)	Lucky: $8 1-year Subscription (D... - San Francisco Union Squar	5:22 am
Bloomspot	Lucky: $8 1-year Subscription (Delivered)	$35 Cut, $145 Brazilian Blowout (Union Sq) - San Francisco Delivered Lucky	5:21 am
Banana Republic	30% savings: the countdown ends soon! - Don't miss an email! Add us to your address book: bananarepublic@email.bana!	5:15 am
WebMD	7 Super Exercises - Diet Reviews: The Instinct Diet Weight Loss Wisdom Saturday, March 23, 2013 woman exercising 7 Supe	5:12 am
Pottery Barn Kids	SAVE 20% on select beach towels & wraps + they all ship FREE - Save 20% on select beach towels and wraps + free ship;	5:05 am
iBookstore	wedding Spring Books Preview - iBookstore Spotlight: Spring Books Preview Some of the most hotly anticipated releases of	4:47 am
Dr. Dennis Gross Skincare	Ferulic Acid - Why It's Our Fave! - Having trouble viewing this message? Try viewing it as a web page. Make sure you receiv	3:02 am

FIGURE 4.1   Email Marketers Compete For Your Time Early Morning

There is a very low probability that someone's going to read through each of these offers. And you can expect more than triple this volume on weekdays. All of these emails are sent by email marketers trying to vie for the same attention you're after. In fact, most of the emails in the figure remained unread by the end of the day Saturday (and probably stayed that way).

People don't read emails that they receive overnight because most people are sleeping. You typically get your highest engagement of reads and clicks within the first hour of delivery, so sending your email overnight already puts you at a disadvantage. Most consumer marketing emails are sent on Tuesdays, Wednesdays, and Thursdays. The highest read rates tend to be either mid-morning or mid-afternoon, with the highest click-through rates consistently being in the mid-afternoon. Interestingly enough, emails sent over the weekend tend to have higher engagement (or click-through rate) but with a lower average read rate, so you're reaching a smaller pool of more engaged prospective customers.

Of course, every business's customer and prospect base is different. Therefore, you'll want to select a starting point to test and validate depending on your goals and the channels you choose to deliver your message. However, keep in mind that because mobile devices have become a staple in our everyday lives, it's becoming less urgent to target a specific time of day. It's far more crucial to ensure that your message will stand out among the others, no matter what time of day, week, or month you're trying to get your target segment's attention.

There are several other critical aspects of timing to consider. For instance, how much advance notice should you give for a sale in order to balance awareness, urgency, and conversion? Or, on the flip side, how *little* notice should you give your customers for last minute offers and still get the highest return? The short answer is that you won't know until you test it out. You might find that your offers hit or miss with return rate in the beginning. However, it shouldn't take long for you to get a feel for when customers are most responsive.

Below are some recommended starting points for when to publish offers based on the time of year, holidays, and events. Note that all of the holidays used in this table are observed in the United States. In a bit, we'll talk about how to optimize by channel.

Seasonality
Spring	Spring cleaning is often a popular extended topic of promotions during this time; you can take advantage of this by promoting a multipart campaign that highlights services and products to be booked anytime. Also, because families often have to contend with spring break and need to plan things out around having the kids at home, it's a good idea to help parents along by giving them more advanced notice than usual for major events (e.g., if you're hosting or sponsoring a Spring Harvest Festival and are trying to get community participation from local families, start promoting it six weeks out). Also, don't forget that many families take time off for spring break, so either plan ahead or take advantage of the kids being home from school.
Summer	Because summertime activities tend to be more lackadaisical and relaxed in general, extend your promotions to last longer. The convenience of being available when the buyer is ready will be a welcome change to the manic winter and spring seasons, in which promotions tend to have specific end dates. A nice program to mix in is ongoing weekly last minute deals throughout the summer; this allows you to draw in consumers when they tend to have more free time

(continued)

Seasonality

Fall	Fall is an interesting time; this is when marketers really start to step on their own feet with holiday promotions. Businesses begin to focus on Thanksgiving the day after Halloween, with no real slowdown until Valentine's Day. Because this is a very heavy time for promotion overload from the larger brands, give yourself an edge by hitting on the less promoted events such as fall harvest, daylight savings, Veteran's Day, and so forth.
Winter	With a wealth of promotional options during this time, put some early thought into what your entire Winter season of offers will look like, and how you're going to spread them out. You want to take care not to flood inboxes and incorrectly set expectations around the frequency of sales during the holiday season, so planning is key. Likely, you'll still have a few last minute deals being published for extra inventory or open appointment slots, so take that into account as well.

Holidays and Events

President's Day, Memorial Day, Martin Luther King, Jr. Day	The flood of promotions tied to these holidays typically starts two to three weeks before the actual holiday, with the biggest marketing push being the week before in an attempt to create a sense of urgency around the sale. This might be a good holiday for small shops to capture some last minute business by leveraging social channels to drive traffic.
Valentine's Day	You have two customer segments to capitalize on here (just like we'll see with the Christmas holiday): planners and procrastinators. You may already have a good idea of your customer makeup when it comes to this. If so, schedule your promotions accordingly. However, most businesses won't be able to forecast customer behavior that accurately; they'll run two

Holidays and Events

	campaigns intended to capture both audiences. You'll want to start in late January to plant the seed for Valentine's Day planners. For the procrastinators, start running last minute weeklies through email and social channels the first week of February. Then, ramp up to daily postings through social channels one week before the actual holiday.
Tax season	The biggest time for tax-related promotions tends to be the first two weeks of April. Get ahead of the heavy marketing push by sending early planning tips and promotions that tie back to the tax season (e.g., "The sooner you do your taxes, the earlier you receive your refund" or "Complete your refund? Let us know and tax is on us!").
Easter	Easter is another holiday that tends to have more planning tied to the holiday weekend itself, so try to send your promotions out at least a few weeks in advance. You may also find a higher conversion rate if your specials and events are scheduled to take place *before* the holiday itself (e.g., "The Easter bunny is visiting us before things get busy! Come by for free photos!").
Mother's Day	This is a great holiday for small and big businesses alike. Start reminding customers and prospects up to a month in advance with ideas more than offers; then transition into a mix of offers and gift card promotions as you get closer to the date. Mother's Day is also a perfect time to leverage last minute campaigns through social and email channels to get those procrastinating gift-givers.

(continued)

Holidays and Events

Father's Day	Father's Day is unique from Mother's Day because the *what* is often very different. However, the marketing cycle tends to be fairly similar in the end. This is a great opportunity to run last minute inventory pushes through social channels.
Independence Day	This holiday tends to spur a lot of long weekend activities and family travel. It's therefore a good plan to provide advance notice for events you're supporting around this time, and promote discounts and activities that help families prepare for the holiday itself.
Labor Day	For many marketers, Labor Day represents a heavy push toward back to school. You may want to consider marketing products and services that are less traditional around the same time (e.g., a spa or salon can say "Congratulations for making it through the summer! Send your kids back to school and pamper yourself.")
Halloween	If you don't have anything particularly relevant to promote for this holiday, we recommend you actually jump off the marketing bandwagon here and use this as an opportunity to build relationships. Take a photo of your team in their Halloween costumes from last year and let your community know a few days in advance that you'll be handing out treats to those who stop by during the evening trick-or-treat run.
Veteran's Day	This holiday has particular significance for many people in the United States, so take this as an opportunity to say thanks to those who served our country, as well as their families. The marketing communication timing should be in line with President's Day or Memorial Day.

Holidays and Events

Thanksgiving	If you don't have anything particularly relevant to incentivize for this holiday, you can do what you did with Halloween and use this time to build relationships. Take the opportunity to simply say thanks to your customers a day or two before the actual day. If you want to use this holiday to drive revenue, consider using online channels for a promotion during the entire month of November for which a percentage of every purchase is donated to a local charity. This type of promotion also extends nicely through the remainder of winter.
Christmas	Over the past few years, marketers have started to employ different Christmas marketing series, with the 12 days of Christmas being the most commonly used. The beauty of this kind of series is that consumers expect to hear from you daily with a different offer that's good up until Christmas Day. The challenge with this kind of series is that you need to spend the time to design the entire program upfront.
New Year's	With the short time frame between Christmas and New Year's (as well as the fact that many consumers have already experienced marketing fatigue and may be on vacation), you might consider sticking to last minute "pamper yourself" deals highlighting the fact that "you made it through another holiday season!" This is the perfect holiday to redirect the focus on one's self and have a good time doing it.

As you probably noticed, there are some repeating patterns with frequency, urgency, and usage of last minute promotions to drive traffic to your business. The timing involved in sending promotions isn't rocket science; however, there are definite nuances specific to your customer and prospect base that you need to figure out over time.

In the end, it's the combination of the 4 Ws—who, what, why, and when—that creates the optimal marketing campaign. Ignoring just one of these puts you and your business at risk not only for compromising your potential return, but also for gaps in information and customer perception that arise from incomplete offers.

Now that you have some ideas for promotions, as well as for their general timing, the next chapter discusses some optimization tips for email and social marketing channels so you can do everything in your power to get the highest conversion possible.

CHAPTER 5

Optimization Tips for Email and Social Marketing

Now that you have an idea of promotions you can run, as well as some segmentation and timing options, we can discuss best practices for optimizing delivery by marketing channel. You've likely heard the term *best practices* before; these are simply recommendations based on industry standards that evolve over time. And because you can read entire books and even take college courses on how to optimize each of these marketing channels, consider the tips in this chapter the abridged version to help get you started. In addition, keep in mind that although best practices are a great place to start, you should still validate that the practice delivers the desired results for *your* specific business.

EFFECTIVE EMAIL MARKETING

Email marketing has become a standard when it comes to scalable, cost-effective marketing solutions for businesses big and small alike. Consumers have also shown marketers year after year that they will continue to engage with businesses through email as long as these messages meet a set of criteria:

- The emails are only sent if a customer opts-in (I want to hear from this business).
- The messages must have content that is engaging and relevant to the consumer (I'm interested in what this business has to say).
- The email messages drive action (I know what to do when I read this email, and I want to do it).

Let's review the basic elements required to effectively leverage this channel and turn your online followers to offline buyers.

Email Subject Line

Far too many businesses spend 99 percent of their energy building fantastic content in their emails, and throw it away in an email subject line that's merely an afterthought. The subject line serves as the gatekeeper between your potential customer and all that great content. You don't have to be especially witty in your email subject lines to get the reader interested; in fact, the more direct you are, the better. Here are some quick tips on how to formulate an effective subject line:

- **Keep it short.** Many email clients will only preview between 40 and 60 characters, so be as concise as possible. If your subject line is too long it won't display in its entirety in the recipient's email inbox, and customers will have to click through to read the rest.
- **Be direct.** Tell your readers what they get out of reading your email. Again, there's no need to be witty here, but if you can get your message across *and* be witty, then go for it.
- **Create a sense of urgency.** Talk about time in a direct but non-aggressive manner. Words like *hurry, now*, and *must* come off as pushy and may not necessarily get the kind of reaction you're looking for from your readers. Instead, use softer words like *reminder* or *overdue*, or create urgency by defining a specific time period (e.g., "one day only" or "last minute").
- **Use numbers.** Using numbers is a great way to be specific and save space. For instance, the phrase "5 At-Home Remedies to Brighten Your Skin Tone" is informational, highlights great content, and saves space with a 5 instead of *Five*. Using numbers to denote discounts can also be extremely effective (e.g., "20% off"). However, be careful not to use them too frequently, because then you run the risk of training your customers to expect a discount and never buy retail.
- **Highlight great content.** If you know content resonates with your readers, don't be afraid to highlight what you've got in store for them. Educational campaigns tend to receive very high engagement when the content is relevant to the recipient.
- **Reinforce open action items.** Email can be a very effective way to remind people they are supposed to complete an action. For instance, Figure 5.2 shows a reminder email from Subaru to take a vehicle in for service.

- **Use words that denote an existing investment.** When used in the right context, words like *your* in the subject line imply that you've already invested something into this business relationship. The email is this business's way of delivering something you want or implying that you've already invested time, energy, or money into the e-mail's subject matter.

- **Personalize the subject line somehow.** There are mixed opinions about how effective it is to include first name personalization in your email subject lines. However, when you can use it in an engaging and *truly* personal manner (as opposed to something that feels displaced and impersonal, such as "Annie, try this now!"), this approach can effectively increase reader conversion.

- **Ask a question.** Engage your readers by asking a question in the subject line so they click through to find out *why* you asked in the first place.

The most effective subject lines are some combination of the tips above. See Figures 5.1 through 5.6 for some examples to get your creative juices flowing.

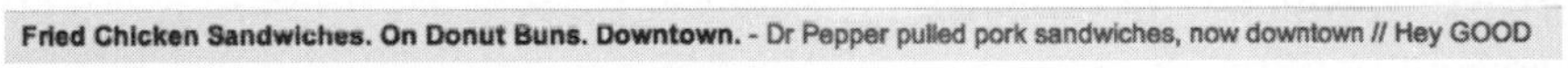

Fried Chicken Sandwiches. On Donut Buns. Downtown. - Dr Pepper pulled pork sandwiches, now downtown // Hey GOOD

FIGURE 5.1 Short, Fun, Witty, and Direct Email Subject Line

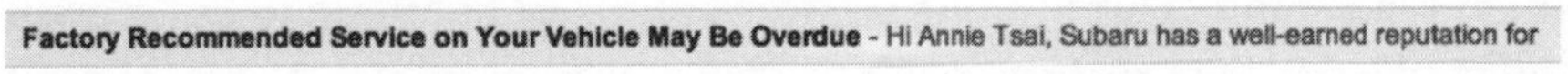

Factory Recommended Service on Your Vehicle May Be Overdue - Hi Annie Tsai, Subaru has a well-earned reputation for

FIGURE 5.2 Direct, Short, and Informational Subject Line That Creates a Sense of Urgency

Top news for Annie: I Learned a Lifetime of Lessons in the Past Year - Top content you're following on LinkedIn LinkedIn Top C

FIGURE 5.3 Subject Line Personalized by Content and Name

Tournament Pick'em Deadline Reminder - Yahoo! Sports Hello, You are receiving this email because the deadline to make last

FIGURE 5.4   Subject Line That Reinforces Open Action Items

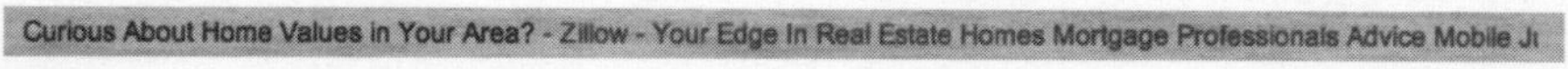

Curious About Home Values in Your Area? - Zillow - Your Edge In Real Estate Homes Mortgage Professionals Advice Mobile Jt

FIGURE 5.5   Ask a Question to Drive the Click

Your 20% off one single item in-store savings certificate is here! - TO PRINT YOUR 20% OFF ONE SINGLE ITEM IN-STORE S

FIGURE 5.6   Direct and Effective Use of _Your_

Don't be afraid to experiment with your email subject lines; you never know what will resonate with your specific customer base. And try to mix things up every few months. Recycled email subject lines get stale very quickly. They also suggest to the reader that there may not be new content for them to consume (or a new action for them to take).

Content Is Still King

After you've gotten your readers to click on the email, you need to have them read it and, if applicable, do what you're asking them to do. A great email doesn't just inform readers about a killer offer; it can remind past customers about what an incredible experience they had when they interacted with your brand and business. Here are some tips to keep in mind when creating email content that draws your customers back to your business:

- **Short and sweet:** In general, the shorter and more to the point you can make your emails, the better your results will be. If you have a lot of content you want to deliver to your customers, consider using the email as an advertisement for it and then delivering the content itself via your website. This will not only allow you to test what kind of content drives the most traffic to your website, but it also has the added benefit of actually getting customers to your website so you can serve up other great content and offers to them.

- **A quick read:** In an ideal world, the reader can consume your emails in a maximum of 30 seconds. Even with a good amount of text included in your email, you can creatively inject images to make sure the message gets across in case the reader doesn't have the time to actually read your entire email. Another way to think about this is to consider how many times it takes for you to scroll your mouse down to reach the bottom of the email. Any more than two scrolls and your email is probably too long to consume in 30 seconds, unless it's entirely comprised of images (which is against best practice).

- **Call to action:** You need to make it as easy as possible for your reader to know the action you want them to take. All of the default appointment reminder emails we send on behalf of our customers have a single call to action in the form of a large button centered in the message asking consumers to electronically confirm their appointments. It's great to have several links and options in your email, but there should be no more than a few specific calls to action.

- **Physical location and contact information:** Make it as trouble-free as possible for the reader to find you if he or she just wants to hop in the car and head over to your business. Any information about your location should be crystal clear and, if possible, include a link that goes directly to an online map so the reader can easily get directions.

- **Tone, grammar, punctuation, and colloquialisms:** The tone and language you use in your emails should reflect your business's personality. If you are a family run business and treat your customers like your family, then don't be afraid to use a more familial or personal tone. Regardless of tone, however, you must *always* use correct grammar and punctuation.

If there are certain colloquialisms you're certain your general population of customers will understand, feel free to inject them into your language. But if there's any question, it's better to be safe than sorry and avoid using these. Typically, colloquialisms and slang have a tendency to sound negative, so here are a few more positive American colloquialisms that might be appropriate to use in your emails given the right context:

- "In a New York minute"
- "Get with the program"
- "Chill" (as in to "chill out for summer")
- "Make waves" (as in "cause a scene")
- "Bad," meaning "good"
- "Red hot" or "on fire" (as in "This sale is red hot!")
- "Blown away"
- "Up for grabs"
- "No worries"
- "Kicks" (as in shoes)
- "Flick" (as in movie)
- "Pick-me-up"
- "Freebie"

- **Images:** Use images to tell your story; but don't use images as your entire email. You need to have a reasonable mix of visual elements and text; otherwise, your email may get flagged as possible spam. In addition, make sure all the images click through to a landing page. If you don't have specific landing pages set up for specific email campaigns, then have them click through to the appropriate page on your website.
- **Multiple formats:** Most email marketing tools will automatically format and send both HTML and text emails for you (Multi-part messaging). Some require you to specify the "text" piece of the email content before you send. If this is the case with the tool you're using, it's always a good idea to review the text body content prior to sending to your customers.

Your call to action will vary depending on your type of business and the purpose of your message. For instance, your goal for one message might be to have your readers connect with you on Facebook. You might use another to try to encourage them to take advantage of some excess inventory. In another, you might try to increase registrations and donations for a community charity event your business is sponsoring. Regardless of what you want readers to do, put some thought into how you are going to display that call to action—that is, where you'll display it in relation to the rest of the email content. And, whether it's a button, an image, or a text link, make sure your readers clearly understand what they should be doing.

Be Aware of the Fold

The *fold* is a term pulled from the newspaper world that refers to just that—the physical fold of the newspaper. The most critical information in this context is always presented "above the fold." This content needs to be catchy enough to draw passersby and entice them to convert from a browser to a buyer. In the email world, everything above the fold is what the reader can see without having to scroll down. This space is typically between 300 and 600 vertical pixels, depending on the reader's screen resolution, the email client being used, and the device being used to read the email.

Most emails these days contain so much content that they require anywhere between one and three scrolls to see the entire message. This number increases on mobile devices and tablets due to their smaller screen sizes. Therefore, staying true to "the fold" gets tricky. Instead of drawing a line across your emails at 400 pixels and designing all of your content to appear above that line, it's probably a better idea to ensure that the most critical information—displayed in the form of email subtitle, one or two sentences, or image—is located toward the top before the reader has to scroll down. This gives your message the best chance of having people both read and act upon the information contained therein. Try to have the following components clearly placed for your readers toward the top of your emails:

- **Logo:** Include your business logo that links to your website or the online business page of your choice. Even though your email will be from your business, you should reinforce the brand awareness. Your logo serves as a great reminder of this.
- **Call to action:** Provide some way for your readers to convert (or click) to where you're trying to get them to go. This could be an image that links to your appointment page or another page on your website, or just to your website itself to display your address and map.
- **Engage:** Indicate what readers can expect if they decide to read on. This plays two roles. First, it fulfills your objective of having the readers consume your email's contents and get excited about what

you're saying and offering. Second, and more important, whatever content you put toward the top of your email should theoretically be enough to trigger a click-through to the destination you've selected.

Use the fold as a guideline to help you to make the tougher choices about email and content design. Keep things simple and focused on getting your message across and getting the reader to click, call, or buy.

Email Marketing Regulations

In the United States, the CAN-SPAM Act of 2003 is the primary regulation to which you must adhere. Almost all email marketing tools will take care of most of this for you, but it's important to note the following requirements for your marketing emails as you are still ultimately responsible for making sure your marketing communications remain compliant. Here are a few things to watch out for:

- **Unsubscribe or preference management options:** Every single email you send that's considered "marketing" needs to include the ability to unsubscribe, opt-out, or manage email preferences.
- **Specific "from" information:** When you send email through an email marketing tool, you're often asked to provide your "from name and from email address." This is called a *vanity from*, and is necessary when an email marketing company sends the email on your behalf. You must own the email address provided and identify the business in a way that the recipient will clearly know from whom the email is coming.
- **Accurate subject lines:** Make sure you provide descriptive yet accurate subject lines. False representation in your subject line could be considered a violation of the CAN-SPAM Act. For instance, your email subject line shouldn't say "50% off today only" if the email content does not reference anything of that nature.
- **Physical address:** Every single email needs to have your current and actual business address that meets postal regulations.

If you find that the marketing emails you're sending somehow do not adhere to the guidelines noted above or those in the CAN-SPAM Act, you should immediately stop sending emails to your customers and contact your email marketing provider to assist you in ensuring compliance.

Avoid Being "Spammy"

All email clients—Gmail, Yahoo!, Hotmail, corporate email servers, and so on—employ a slightly different algorithm through which they put every single email they receive. This algorithm's job is to determine whether they should consider that email to be spam. Emails that are flagged as spam get automatically filtered out of the inbox, typically to the Spam or Bulk folder. Even though spam filters have gotten much more sophisticated over the past several years, some legitimate business, marketing, and personal emails still get flagged as spam and end up being filtered.

It's therefore crucial that you follow a few easy guidelines that will help you do everything in your power to get into your customers' inboxes:

- **Well-formatted HTML:** Your emails are coded in HTML, or Hyper-Text Markup Language. If you are using an email marketing tool to create your HTML messages, it's likely that your outbound emails are already formatted well. If you are having your own designers code your email templates for you or are designing emails yourself in WYSIWYG software like Dreamweaver, then you need to make sure your HTML is clean. The World Wide Web Consortium, or W3C, offers a free HTML validator at http://validator.w3.org.
- **Avoid "spam trap" words:** Because the email subject line acts as the gateway to your email, a message is often filtered if the subject line contains spammy words. Your email text content will also be scanned. Your email's overall spam "score" will determine whether the message gets filtered out of the inbox.

  Here are some words and phrases to avoid, as they tend to flag your emails as spam:
  - Free/FREE
  - See for yourself
  - All natural
  - No obligation
  - Full refund
  - 50% off
  - Satisfaction guaranteed

- Giving away
- Get it now
- 100%
- Offer expires
- You have been selected
- Act now!
- #1
- Special promotion
- Affordable
- No cost
- Weight loss/lose weight
- Instant
- Accept credit cards
- Call now
- Great offer
- Save up to. . .

There are hundreds of words and phrases that are known to trigger spam filtering, and every email provider has a different variation of that list. It's nearly impossible to predict exactly what words you should avoid in order to guarantee inbox placement. Just try to stay away from the big offenders and focus instead on ensuring your content is relevant and your subject lines are optimized.

- **Reasonable image-to-text ratio:** The ratio of text content to image content in your email messages is frequently the reason that emails are flagged as spam. Small businesses too often try to take a scanned image of an offline flyer and drop it in an email. You need to have a reasonable ratio of text to images, with about 60 percent text. Reducing the size of your images may also help.

The other and perhaps more important reason to have enough text in your email content is that most email providers today will automatically turn images off unless the email recipient has previously stated they want to view images from you. If your email is a single large image or several smaller ones with a lack of descriptive "alt" text (alternative text displays can be used in place of images when images are disabled and can be entered for most images when using an email marketing tool to build your emails), then your email recipient sees what is shown in Figure 5.7 above the fold, instead of what is shown in Figure 5.8.

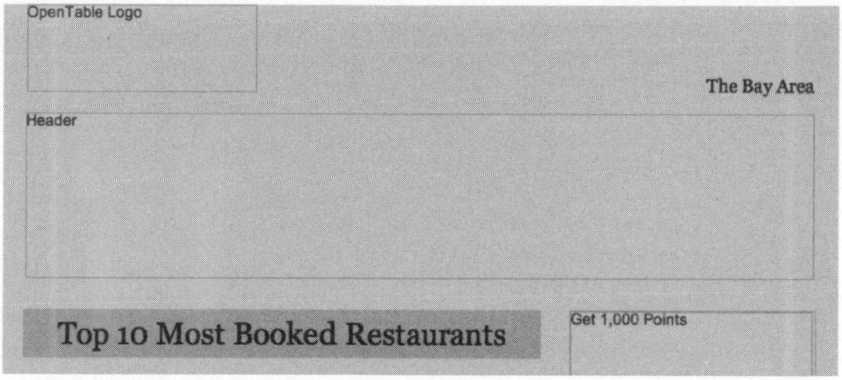

OpenTable Logo
The Bay Area
Header
Top 10 Most Booked Restaurants
Get 1,000 Points

FIGURE 5.7 Email with Images Disabled (with Alt Text)

OpenTable
The Bay Area
Diners' Choice
This month's top ten lists as voted by diners like you.
See All Lists
Top 10 Most Booked Restaurants
Get 1,000 Points with 1 Reservation

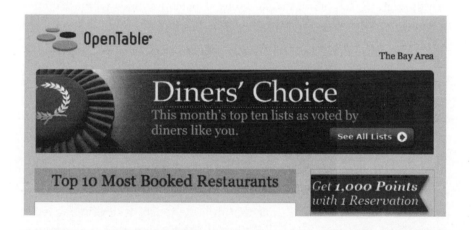

FIGURE 5.8 Email with Images Enabled

- **Excessive punctuation and use of symbols:** Though this seems fairly obvious, it's still worth mentioning. You don't need four exclamation marks to denote your own excitement or the fact that your email recipients should be excited. Use of proper grammar, punctuation, and symbols is both a crucial part of delivering the right tone to your email recipients *and* avoiding being flagged as spam. Stay true to the voice you've decided to use on behalf of your business, and you'll be just fine.

Email marketing is an extremely effective and scalable way to communicate with your audience in a personalized and creative manner. When done right, it can generate some of the highest returns on your marketing dollar. Focus on planning out the right offers for your target audience and implementing some of the best practices discussed in this section to put your message in the best position to get into the inbox, get read, and convert readers to buyers. Don't be afraid to test things out with your customers and find the right mix of offers to conversation. Most importantly, have some fun with it!

OPTIMIZING YOUR SOCIAL CHANNELS

In this section, we discuss some general best practices when it comes to engaging with your audience via social channels. You can apply all of the best practices listed here across most social channels, but I point out some platform-specific tips when it comes to profile completeness. It's important to note here that using social channels to create enhanced customer engagement does not *immediately correlate* to a high revenue return. But once you build up your audience, and your platform-specific community is actively engaging with your business, it becomes significantly easier to leverage this channel to convert business. For instance, once you are able to build a community of followers on Facebook, last-minute offers are a great approach that performs very well. Until then, use the tips that follow to start developing your community and generating the kind of interaction that will produce long-term results.

Be Where Your Community Is

Luckily for you and for other businesses looking to understand where they should focus their social marketing efforts, we can narrow a great deal of it down to one site. Facebook represents almost half of the time consumers are spending on social networking. However, that doesn't necessarily mean that Facebook is the right place for you to focus your energy. I pointed out earlier that it's critical that you understand where your customers spend *their* time, which you can determine by using the customer survey template in Chapter 2 or another survey you choose. You might uncover that your community loves Pinterest, Twitter, Foursquare, Google+, or some other platform, and that's where you should target your marketing efforts. Until you ask you'll never know, and you risk spending time optimizing the wrong social platform.

Wherever you decide to focus, you'll want to direct your efforts on building awareness about the fact that you're using this channel as an engagement tool within your customer community. Update your website, business cards, all of your emails, and other marketing collateral to easily identify on which social channels you're spending your time. You might have a little more space within your website and emails to educate your visitors on the benefit of joining your social community (e.g., get great last minute offers, learn about how they can participate in community events, etc.). Most social platforms will provide icons that you can use on your website and in your emails. Or, you can Google "social media icons" and find the ones that have been dressed up and match the style you desire.

Complete Your Profile

This section will provide a bit more information for some major social platforms. Each one we discuss allows you to complete and customize your profile so your followers can get to know your business better. And a benefit to effectively optimizing your profiles and accounts is that you may see improvements in your search results over time. Keep in mind that social platforms evolve very quickly, so I'm going to focus on general optimization as opposed to targeting recent changes. Below are some tips specific to each social channel that you'll want to leverage when creating a complete profile.

Facebook Facebook has made several changes to their page layout over the past few years, which can pose a challenge for small businesses trying to keep up with the current trends. In addition, Facebook will likely continue to make adjustments to their design over the course of the next several years, so it will be important for you as a business to understand how these changes affect your ability to engage with your customers. But regardless of what your Facebook page looks like today or tomorrow, there are some time-tested optimization tips that you should implement:

- **Make sure you create a business page that is separate from your personal profile.** Many of our customers start off on Facebook with a personal page and end up driving their professional followers there. Once they realize this mistake, they need to figure out how to migrate their existing followers to their new business page so they can take advantage of that feature. It's much better to keep them separate from the very beginning. You can do that by going to www.facebook.com/pages/create. Make sure you select "Local Business or Place" if you are a small business (see Figure 5.9).

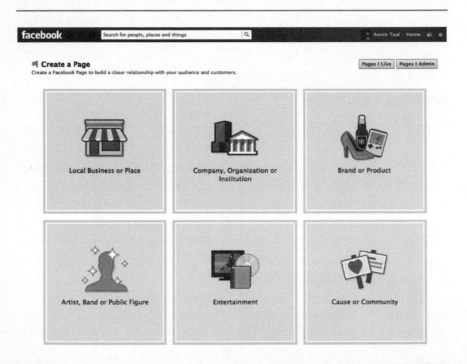

FIGURE 5.9   Create a Business Page on Facebook

- **Get a vanity URL.** If you haven't done this yet, it's critical that you do. Having a vanity URL makes it easy for prospective customers and your social community to find you. For example, Demandforce's Facebook URL is www.facebook.com/demandforce. You can create your vanity URL by going to www.facebook.com/username.
- **Update your "About" section.** Make sure this information is accurate and comprehensive. The details you provide in this section will become increasingly important as Facebook introduces more advanced search capabilities. You may also find that great "About" descriptions improve search results over time. Demandforce's "About" section is shown in Figure 5.10.
- **Backfill your timeline.** Your Facebook timeline allows you to enter business milestones of your choice. It's a great tool to build credibility for your business among those who aren't necessarily familiar with your brand. You don't need to do this right away, but you should eventually

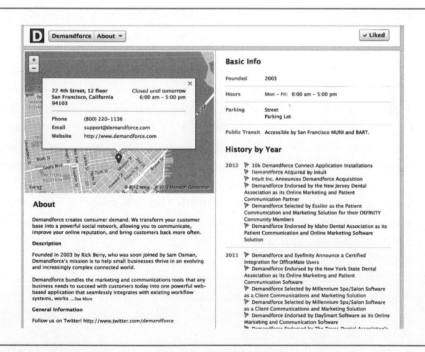

FIGURE 5.10   Facebook "About" Section

take the time to update your business page with this information. Here's a list of events that you may want to consider adding to your timeline:

- Add an event for when you opened for business or incorporated.
- Add events for any major expansions or remodels that customers would've noticed.
- If you changed locations or physical addresses, add events for each to indicate growth.
- If you tracked when you reached a certain customer count, create events for each of those milestones.
- If you have a longtime employee who is a cornerstone for the business, highlight when he or she started working there (including any very important pets that are a part of your work family).
- If you sponsor a community event, add a timeline event for every year you participated.
- If you are a family-run business, create an event for when a specific cherished family member joined the team.
- If you're proud of how long you've been delivering a specific service or offering a specific product, add an event for when you started making it available.
- If you sponsor a local sports team, add an event for both your sponsorship as well as any milestones that team has accomplished.
- If you have specific long-time customers that are well known in your community, add an event for when they made their first purchases with you. One tip about backfilling your Facebook timeline: Once you start adding historical events, Facebook no longer displays when you actually signed up for an account with this social site.

- **Connect your Facebook page to *all* the other social platforms you use, such as Twitter, Pinterest, Instagram, Foursquare, Yelp, and so on.** This is an easy way to ensure fresh content regularly appears on your page. This will also help you build awareness around the other social networks where you decide to spend time on your business's behalf. If you find that your Facebook page is getting bombarded with questionably relevant content, it's just as easy to stop the feed anytime.
- **Tag people in as many photos as you can, whether they're of customers, family members, employees, or anyone else.** There are two benefits here: (1) You can't tag someone on Facebook

unless they are following the business, so it's an easy way to increase followership (e.g., "Like my Facebook page so I can tag you in this great photo!"), and (2) Every tagged photo gets shared to the tagged person's Facebook page as well, which will increase your reach.

There will be countless other options for optimizing your business page as Facebook continues to evolve. The reality, though, is it doesn't really matter how optimized your business page is; if your content isn't genuine and engaging to the point that your community is liking, commenting on, and sharing your posts, you've got to go back to the drawing board.

Twitter Your Twitter profile is made up of four main sections: your identifier (name and Twitter handle), your photo, your description, and your background. Each element plays a role in delivering information to your users and the web, so follow these tips to maximize results:

- Use your business name or your full name in the title. Twitter likes real people having real conversations.
- Try a Twitter username that includes the business name and some indicator for geographic location. For instance, BodyRok, located in San Francisco, uses the Twitter username @bodyroksf. Or, doctors may prefer that their Twitter usernames be their name as opposed to business name (e.g., @drspok versus @southbeachdental).
- If you're representing yourself personally, and not your business, use a photo of a real person. If the account is for your business, use your logo or a photo that will represent the business in the small space allotted. Twitter browsers will be able to view the image in full size if they click on the image itself, but they likely won't. Use your actual name or your business name as the image filename (e.g., AnnieTsai.jpg).
- Keep the description succinct and focus on keywords that are clear for both readers and search engines. You have 160 characters to tell your story. You can use hashtags here (e.g., #SanFrancisco) if you want, but it's not necessary. It's more important to use this section to let potential followers know what they can expect from you if they choose to connect. Your description also plays an important role for Twitter search engines and algorithms when they are looking for other Twitter users to recommend.

- Your Twitter page's background image gives you an opportunity to get a little creative. There are two background images you can personalize—the one that displays behind your profile content and the main image on your profile page itself. Figure 5.11 shows a Twitter page with a grey-tone general page design for the personal page, with the two backgrounds closely matching. This page primarily highlights a blog title and logo.

For Demandforce's Twitter page, we've gone with a deep blue background and created a left aligned "tweet roll" to highlight the various Tweeters we have at the company (see Figure 5.12).

You've got a number of options with your background image, so don't be afraid to have some fun with it.

However, you don't want to get too creative when designing your Twitter page, since the busier the page looks, the more the eye will be drawn away from the conversation itself. Twitter is an engagement tool, so concentrate in the beginning on making sure you're broadcasting great content.

Pinterest Several of the optimization tips for Pinterest profile completion are similar to Facebook and Twitter. However, I do think it's worth going into a bit of detail for why they are particularly important on your Pinterest business pages:

- **Company username:** You have 15 characters to create an optimized username. Because most company names won't fit, pick a shortened

FIGURE 5.11   Personal Twitter Page

FIGURE 5.12   Business Twitter Page

name that is perhaps the same as your Twitter profile name or is a shorthand business name that you've already been using for a while. **Your website**: This adds a layer of legitimacy to your business page, so get your business URL into your Pinterest account information and click that "verify website" button!

- **Your "about" profile:** You have 200 characters here to describe your business and let users know why they should follow you through this social channel. Use accurate and descriptive keywords to tell your story. Figure 5.13 shows a great example of a short and sweet profile from Fusion Spa Salon Aveda in Florida (http://pinterest .com/fusionspasalon/).

FIGURE 5.13   Pinterest "About" Page

- **Link with every Pin:** If you're pinning images of products and services that customers can order or have completed by your business, be sure to include a link to the purchase page in the Pin's description. If relevant, include your appointment or quote request links to drive business to your website or preferred landing page. For instance, Fusion Spa Salon Aveda in Florida has a well laid out and comprehensive Pinterest page (http://pinterest.com/fusionspasalon/) that focuses on both style and rewards for customers. Every image links back to either their website, their Facebook page, the original referring pin, or a specific landing page that is tied to the offer or contest being advertised.
- **Keyword friendly and specific board names:** The default boards are For the Home, My Style, and Products I Love. You will get literally *thousands* of results if you search for "things I love" on Pinterest. You want to differentiate your Pinboards by giving them descriptive names. For instance, one of our salon customers pins photos of great hairstyles to various Pinboards by event type—Prom Hairstyles, Red Carpet Hairstyles, Date Night Hairstyles, and so forth. You can also have a board for each geographic location if you have multiple locations for your business.
- **Optimize image filenames:** It works in much the same way as your Twitter profile picture: images that are optimized with true descriptions of the file will improve the way your business's content displays in image search results. Also, make sure you are uploading your own images as well as sharing other Pinterest users' images so you can improve the viral aspect of your own Pinboards over time.
- **Pin regularly:** Whatever your social publication schedule, make sure you are pinning regularly. Weekly or biweekly is a great place to start.

Although Pinterest is a newer site to many small businesses, there are several relevant applications of this social channel that make a lot of sense if you're willing to invest the time. If you're interested in Pinterest but don't want to commit to it as a business tool, try starting a personal Pinterest page first, connect it to your Facebook account, and give it a test drive.

Profile completeness is a combination of several factors: providing the right level of information to your readership, delivering some important information for search optimization, and leveraging the various platform-specific tools to most effectively engage with your community. Although social platforms will introduce new versions and redesigns every so often, the basic premise still holds true: make sure that those who have chosen to connect with you via that social platform are able to get to know and engage with your business effortlessly.

Brevity Is Better

In the world of social media, the fewer words you use to communicate your message, the better your chances of increasing engagement levels. Just because a social platform allows for a certain number of characters doesn't mean you need to use all of them. Facebook's limit for posts is 60,000 characters; however, the site's analysis shows that those between 100 to 250 characters will yield 60 percent more engagement than posts with more than 250 characters. You want to try to stay below 100 characters on Twitter.

Google+, however, is on the other end of the spectrum. This site allows 100,000 characters per post. Due to the nature of this platform, and Google's intent for Google+ to allow businesses and users to generate deeper levels of engagement with smaller circles than the other social networks out there, more content may be preferable here. However, as it is with all other endeavors, you'll never know until you try and see what your customers respond to best.

Increase Engagement with Images, Video, and Questions

Studies have repeatedly shown that regardless of social platform, highly engaging, relevant, and entertaining content provides a winning formula. The key to providing this is to offer posts that are a blend of information, promotion, and just plain fun, as seen in Figure 5.14. Mixing content up keeps things fresh on your social platforms, and keeps customers coming back for more.

Facebook research found that images and videos consistently receive higher engagement in the form of likes, comments, and shares than text alone. Therefore, Facebook decided to give images more real estate when they introduced the newest version of their page design.

Twitter has also enhanced their site over time to show previews and content with images to improve engagement levels (see Figure 5.15).

FIGURE 5.14   Don't Be Afraid to Share Fun Content on Facebook

FIGURE 5.15   Twitter Post With Image Increases Engagement

Across social platforms, images and videos play a critical role in catching and drawing the eye in. Another way to attract browsers is to ask questions to your audience and engage with them through comments. Depending on the community makeup of the social platform, posing questions to your audience can be an extremely effective way to get people to comment on your page. Keep questions short and grammatically correct, and make sure to read them aloud a few times before posting. Too often we write as we talk, which doesn't translate as well to print. Tying questions to images is a great way to both catch the eye and start a conversation (see Figures 5.16 through 5.18).

Social channels give you the opportunity to engage with customers and followers to build interest that converts over time. Make sure you set up the foundation for your business profiles on these social channels by following the tips outlined in this chapter, mixing content up to drive

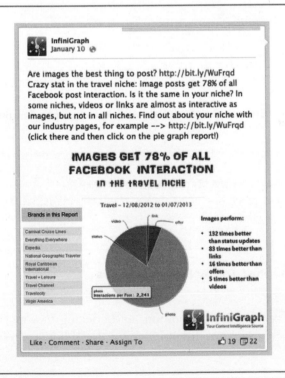

FIGURE 5.16   Lead Content with a Question

FIGURE 5.17 Show a Single Image and Ask an Open-Ended Question

FIGURE 5.18 Post True or False Questions

more than just revenue generation, and sticking to your schedule for post frequency, which we discuss in more detail in the next chapter.

CHAPTER **6**

Activity: Build Your 12-Month Online Marketing Plan

Since we're about halfway through the book at this point, let's review what we've covered so far. You've taken a hard look at the state of your online reputation today in an attempt to understand potential gaps. You've put together a plan to close those gaps, and hopefully you now are on your way to a strong foundation for giving your online browsers the best chance of converting into offline buyers. You've established ways to learn more about your customers in offline and online environments, which will allow you to more effectively target your advertising time and dollars. This will also help you better understand which social channels you should focus on to give you the biggest bang for your time investment.

You've learned about the kinds of programs you can implement to generate both incremental and last-minute business through targeted and segmented offers. You've gotten a feel for the landscape of the types of promotions you can run throughout the year, and perhaps have decided around which holidays or events you will build marketing programs. You understand the basics of optimizing your conversation through email and social marketing with the goal of tapping in to what your potential customers are already doing through those channels, and you are learning what they expect from businesses in terms of engagement.

Now for the fun part! It's time to build your 12-month online marketing plan. This will help you develop a holistic view of how your online marketing efforts are going to drive incremental business. Thus far we haven't talked much about spending in terms of actual dollars. Nearly every investment we've discussed has involved investing time. In this section, I'll also overlay potential add-on spending options so you can get a feel for ways you can nudge your programs along and increase velocity if needed.

DETERMINE YOUR BUSINESS GOALS

Your business goals should drive your 12-month plan's overall strategy; therefore, you need to have a clear idea of what this strategy is. Are you looking to build a foundation for your online and social presence? Or is your primary objective to create a surge in new customers? As you can imagine, your overall program's high-level design will differ greatly depending on your objective. In this chapter, we will create two default marketing plan templates based on the following goals:

1. Build sustainable growth and repeat business
2. Drive surges in new business

Once you're better able to understand the differences in how you can execute your marketing plan based on your business goals, you'll then have a chance to download our 12-month planning worksheet and create your own online marketing plan at the end of this chapter.

ESTIMATE YOUR SPENDING POWER

Before you get into the details of your online marketing plan, make sure you know what your budget is—specifically, what you are currently spending marketing dollars on and how that compares to other small businesses. In December 2012, Ad-ology Research published a study on 1,439 U.S. small businesses with 100 employees or fewer.[1] Of those who responded, 53.5 percent spent greater than $1,000 per year on marketing or advertising, with 30.5 percent stating they planned on spending more in 2013. Those who planned to spend more were primarily targeting online and mobile marketing and direct mail, whereas those planning to spend less cited the Yellow Pages, direct mail, and newspapers as channels being targeted.

You might wonder why you should get an idea of what other businesses are doing. Benchmark data like this tells us an interesting story about trends among small businesses that offer very useful lessons. First, small businesses are still spending a significant part of their

---

[1] Ad-ology, ad-ology.com, Small Business Marketing Forecast 2013.

overall marketing budget in direct mail; some business owners are finding enough success to invest more, where others have opted to reduce spending there. As with all marketing channels, the definition of "effectiveness" depends on a number of factors, including geography, target demographic, and of course, program execution. Second, many small businesses haven't figured out how to best leverage the paid aspects of online marketing channels to convert those online browsers to offline customers. That said, about one-third of the small business marketing budget remains allocated to digital, content, or social marketing efforts.

So, what do you spend on marketing and where should you adjust this year? If you don't already catalog your marketing allocation, take a look at your last two months' spending and try to categorize it into the following groups:

- Direct mail
- Email marketing
- Community events, causes, sports, contests
- Content (PR, blogging, video production)
- Social media marketing (social contests, paid ads, promoted ads, apps)
- Digital marketing (website, mobile, online advertising, daily deals)
- Offline print marketing (signage, billboards, trade publications, collateral)
- Broadcast marketing (TV, radio)

Generally, traditional allocation for businesses that focus their primary channels offline might look something like what is shown in Figure 6.1.

In this model, over 70 percent of the marketing allocation is targeted toward general awareness campaigns, offline marketing channels, and community engagement, with the bulk of the remainder allocated toward email marketing efforts.

Now that you have an estimate of how much you're spending by major group, you'll want to understand how effective your current marketing mix is. The next step is to use a scale of 1 through 10 to rate how effective you believe each channel group is (1 being the least effective, 10 being the most). This score may need to be more subjective if you don't have actual data to back your return on investment, but try to tie your score to as much data as possible. If you're surveying your

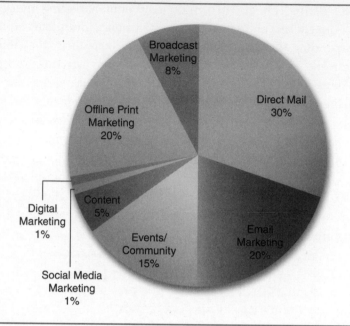

FIGURE 6.1   Current Marketing Allocation

customers, you should have some information on which channels create the most lasting impression among those who are spending money with you. Use this as a starting point if you don't have any other hard data.

It's also important to ask yourself questions along the way. Specifically, if you don't have access to any *real* information on how effective a specific channel is at helping you meet your marketing goals, how much should you *really* be spending there in the first place? This question will help spark a conversation about how to adjust your marketing budget allocation, thereby allowing you to take away from what's not necessarily working in order to test new channels.

We'll use the benchmark data noted above in our marketing plan samples, and base our plan on a $12,000 annual marketing budget ($1,000 per month.) We'll make assumptions on increased and decreased spending based on reallocating away from difficult-to-measure offline channels. It's important to note here that with a relatively small annual marketing budget of $12,000, the percent reallocated toward online channels will likely be larger than if your overall marketing budget were greater. This annual budget might seem like a lot, but to keep things in context, a business with annual revenues of $300,000 can reallocate just 4 percent of the revenue stream toward all of its marketing efforts to realize $12,000.

MARKETING FOR SUSTAINED GROWTH

Generally, businesses that are looking to design their online marketing programs to support sustained growth have already somewhat established themselves in the offline world and have an existing book of business. They are beginning to recognize that having an online reputation is an important investment in the business's long-term health. You can then redesign your initial online marketing strategy to deliver on a trickle of business over time. This will allow it to easily evolve into a relationship development and management tool for your business. Eventually, businesses that successfully leverage social and online channels to manage customer relationships and build a strong following are able to significantly influence bottom line conversion through these channels.

A sustained growth online marketing plan will prompt you to decide where to build on the baseline program you have today. If we account for the current marketing allocation noted above, we know that we want to reallocate some of your budget to online channels. This will give you room to create a great test environment to identify which online channels are most effective for your business. Consider shifting some of your offline or less effective or measurable channels to email marketing, online advertising, and social media to create a more balanced marketing budget.

To review, the old plan was shown in Figure 6.1, and the new plan is shown in Figure 6.2.

Notice that this new marketing budget's main adjustment is to take money almost entirely from broadcast marketing, which is an extremely difficult channel to measure for a return on your investment, or ROI. This money is then reallocated across email, social media, and digital marketing, which will be able to deliver significantly higher measureable return over time. Because you have a $1,000 per month marketing budget, you are effectively reallocating 50 percent to online efforts.

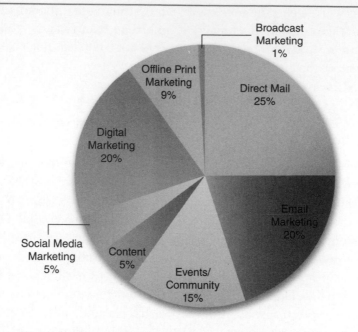

FIGURE 6.2   Proposed Marketing Allocation

Even with the fairly significant budget reallocation, you're still dedicating 15 percent to the community in this new model, and you're spending a majority of your offline budget in direct mail, as you always have. When your marketing budget increases, the total percentage allocated to online marketing channels will significantly decrease since the cost of leveraging these tools scales very well as your business grows. Although many small businesses continue to contribute significant chunks of their total allocation to online channels as their online presence grows, you will likely top out in spending $3,000 to $4,000 per month in the "sustainable growth" model.

Let's assume we have $500 to spend on email marketing, social marketing, online advertising, and content marketing every month. Since our objective is to build a steady stream of business, you're likely going to focus on gaining a certain number of new customers or increasing top-line revenue per month. You can expect a delayed adoption curve from consumers and online browsers in your first few months running campaigns through online channels and getting your programs going. And you're actually going to spend more time than dollars upfront to make sure your online marketing channels are established in ways that will best deliver on your desired outcomes.

Based on these assumptions, Table 6.1 shows a partially filled out 12-month online marketing plan that averages $500 per month for a boutique clothing and accessories store. (Note that you may not need to spend $500 every month.)

Notice that most of this online plan's marketing investment is tied to giveaways or promoting an event on behalf of something you're supporting that also happens to be taking place on your Facebook page or at your store. When you're focusing on social, email, and online marketing as tools to establish relationships and generate incremental return, you'll concentrate heavily during your first year on creating an environment where people want to go because they see your business as a pillar in the community. This message needs to come through in your online assets.

MARKETING FOR HIGH GROWTH

The process of creating a plan that supports a high-growth strategy is very different from the sustained growth plan we just developed. One of the key distinctions is that this strategy focuses your marketing dollars primarily on traffic conversion as opposed to promoting other people or organization's causes and content. (See Figure 6.3.)

In truth, businesses in *all* stages of development find themselves looking for surges in revenue. They could be facing a local recession, finding that they aren't able to consistently sustain the margins they could before, dealing with a product quality or service delivery issue and subsequent customer attrition, or maybe they are just looking to test the waters and heavily expand. Regardless of the reason, make sure that you follow the offer design guidelines noted in earlier chapters and staff people and product sufficiently so you can deliver on a preferred experience and keep those customers coming back.

A high-growth plan requires that you primarily spend your marketing dollars to get people in the door. Perhaps you're losing money or have very little margin on the specific product you've highlighted, but you are

TABLE 6.1   12-Month Online Marketing Plan Sample— Sustained Growth

Month	Month
January°	*February°°*

January°

Theme: Let's Get Healthy Together

Story: This month, we're focusing the online conversation on supporting a healthy community. You'll highlight store products that encourage customers to keep all of those new resolutions they've established, and motivate them to share their resolutions on your Facebook page with a social contest.

Social Contest: Get your friends to support your resolution from our Facebook page. The customer with the most "likes" in January wins a $200 gift card to our store. (Second, third, and fourth runner up prizes will encourage overall activity.)

Social Advertising: Set a $50 advertising limit the first week of January and another $50 the second week in January to promote your social contest.

Website/Content/Email Marketing: Make sure your other online assets have updated text and visuals to drive all traffic to your social campaign.

Direct Mail: If you are planning this program in advance and can incorporate your direct mail strategy here, definitely make sure the content is aligned with your social marketing objectives.

In-Store: Make sure you print up flyers that highlight your social contest and train your staff on how to get customers excited.

°Your objective throughout the month is to increase overall engagement on your Facebook page. Use this additional traffic to test how successful different types of offers are with this segment. Focus on incremental offers of 10 to 15 percent off, highlight specific products on sale, or leverage a more fluid promotions campaign around discounting products that receive high social engagement.

February°°

Theme: Saying I Love You; relationship-building month

Story: Since you kicked off January with a social program intended to increase engagement on your Facebook page, you should now have a fairly active following. Take this month to soften the conversation and focus your promotion on "Gifts That Say I Love You."

Email Marketing: Every week, send your opt-in list an email with highlighted products that say "I love you" for the demographic you are targeting in your store.

Social Media: Leverage Pinterest if you're on the site to get great images to share on your Facebook page. Give your customers creative ways to say "I love you" that they can customize. Highlight products alongside these ideas to drive purchase conversion.

Local Online Directory Advertising: Post an ad on the online directory of your choice for gift cards to catch any last minute spenders. Highlight this offer in-store as well to increase per-visit spending.

°°This month, your objective is to deliver really fantastic content to your social communities and get your new followers hooked.

TABLE 6.1   (Continued)

March and April°

Theme: Supporting Our Local Schools

Story: Take a little break in March and April and combine the two months for a longer-running theme. Highlight the schools you support and engage the community to share photos of students in action during games, school clubs, and extracurricular activity events; selling baked goods to raise money at your store; volunteering at the food bank, and so on. This is an opportunity to focus on how you are giving back to your community and to build a stronger bond with neighborhood families.

Social Advertising: Invest marketing dollars during this time in promoting posts about when sports teams or school clubs are going to be holding events at your store (e.g., bake sale to raise money for new sports equipment).

Email Marketing: Focus email marketing content on ages- and demographic-appropriate products and content along with offers that provide additional discounts to students and parents of the school district to drive additional traffic.

Social Contest: Consider a social contest where the product is something for the schools. For instance, if the sports team is interested in a new logo design, front the prize money and use your Facebook page as the hub for voting.

Website: Create a photo album that highlights the various community events your business supports.

°*Use this time to become an institution in your neighborhood and a known avid supporter of the local schools and the community. Continue to offer incremental deals on products and services, but let the students, teachers, and parents tell their stories about which products they love and why.*

May and June

Theme: Celebrating Mom and Dad

Story: Now that you've got families and schools on board, take these next two months to offer students, families, and schools cost-effective ways to say thanks to the parents who make everything possible.

Social Contest: Weekly $100 gift card drawings for students who share their stories about why their moms or dads should be pampered with a shopping spree at your store.

July°°

Theme: Support a Cause; relationship-building month

Story: The summer months present several opportunities for you to support larger social efforts, nonprofit organizations, fundraisers, and so on.

Online Marketing: The great thing about social and community efforts is that many of them have their own landing pages and methods for collecting donations. You can easily piggy back on top of this by offering to match up to a certain amount for your best customers who are raising money for a cause, or even by simply linking your customers' donation pages to your website and various other online assets.

°°*With the focus on relationship building and continuing to be a foundation within your community, what ways can you leverage online and social marketing to drive support for your chosen cause and get customers through your door?*

August

Theme: Summer of Fun; Heart of Baseball

Story: August is typically a lower marketing spend month for small businesses, so find ways to have some fun with the end of summer and serve as a hub for the community.

Online Marketing: Consider mixing online and offline tactics during the summertime to encourage customers to spend more of their leisure time at your store. For instance, work with your neighboring businesses to host ice cream and other food trucks and put tables and chairs out front to draw a crowd. Leverage all of your online channels to promote the event and offer discounts to those who also purchase food items from the trucks.

TABLE 6.1   (Continued)

Month	Month
September Theme: Back to School; donation center Story: Back to school is a great theme for small businesses. Not only can you leverage the need to update family wardrobes as a revenue driver; you can also become a donation center for less fortunate students and offer a discount for each donation. This shows customers you care about them *and* about helping the community at large. Email and Social Marketing: Leverage these channels to run a month-long theme about why doing business with your business is worth their while. Sprinkle in product offerings specific to back to school and encourage buyers to bring in slightly used clothing that no longer fits their children for donation for a discount on new clothing or other products. Social Advertising: If you have any back to school specific products, consider testing single item promotions to your followers.	*October* Theme: Relationship-building month Story: If you are planning on carrying products for Halloween (or already do), this is an easy planning month. If not, leverage this time to continue relationship building.

November and December

Theme: Not Your Ordinary Holiday; donation center

Story: The holidays are a fantastic time to get creative with promotions. Find ways to get customers to spend leisurely time in your store learning about products, or bring in designers or makeup stylists to prep customers for parties. Emphasize the fact that you are a local store, and evolve your business and employees to become an extension of your customers' families. And don't forget that Small Business Saturday also falls during this time (the Saturday following Thanksgiving), so make sure to take advantage of the national event.

Email Marketing: Invest some dollars into having a holiday look and feel designed to match your store's interior design. Then, simply include photos of products and spaces taken from inside your store to make your emails feel like extensions of your business.

Online Marketing: Leverage the same email images for your website.

Social Contest: Design a contest around giving—the five most shared "holiday wishes" will be in the finals for selection of a $300 to $500 grand prize.

looking to drive incremental revenue through a higher average purchase price per ticket or by securing return business. Here are a few strategies you should consider employing with a high-growth online marketing plan to support those two outcomes:

- Focus on the conversion to the store to give customers the chance to browse and find something special for them. Sometimes, the product

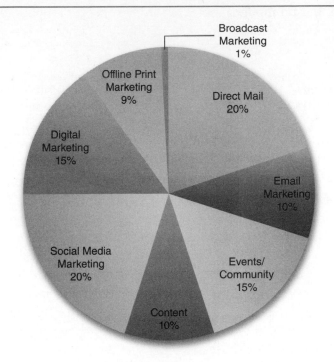

FIGURE 6.3   Proposed Marketing Allocation

you highlight doesn't end up being the one they purchase. Make sure your published offers support this kind of purchase habit.

- You can still have a high-growth strategy and show support for the community, as noted in the March/April examples in Table 6.1. Focus your business's marketing dollars on getting people through the door and then tying purchase discounts to community event participation.
- Take advantage of gifting occasions by offering bundled packages, gift baskets, gift cards, and kits so the buyer doesn't have to think as much about what to buy. Mix high-end and low-cost products in these gift sets to increase overall margin.
- Promote heavy discounts once in a while to draw in a crowd and strategically stock your inventory with low-cost/high-margin items to encourage upsells.

- Target your promotional items toward lower cost or higher discounts to drive clicks, then offer a suite of offerings at all price points that buyers can choose from.

Realistically, you're not likely to be spending an entire year executing on a single strategy. Most businesses ebb and flow throughout the year and need to implement hybrid programs to meet their overall objectives. Given this perspective, make sure that you are building a 12-month online marketing plan that allows for some flexibility to adjust if needed. You may find that you want to get a little more aggressive one month and can slow down the next month.

The beauty of an online marketing plan is that even though you can plan far in advance, you don't need to actually *execute* until much closer to the date. If you find that you need to adapt on the fly and allocate your dollars toward a specific program, you have the freedom to do so.

Now it's your turn. Are you a business looking to leverage online marketing to drive long-term, sustainable growth? Try building a 12-month online marketing plan by downloading the template here: www.wiley.com/go/smallbizhandbook.

CHAPTER **7**

Reduce Overall Marketing Spend: Get Offline Customers Online

Depending on your customer demographic and sometimes your geographic region, your customers may inherently prefer to engage with you in the offline world. In other circumstances, customer preferences may dictate that you naturally market to and mostly interact with your customers online. Regardless of your starting point, the cost of traditional offline marketing—especially with the increases in postage rates— should be incentive enough for you to find its online marketing counterparts attractive. In case you haven't been sold on why you want to put energy into getting your customers online, here are a few other reasons to consider:

- Offline marketing programs typically require significantly more lead time to plan, design, and execute.
- Creative elements for offline print marketing can be significantly more expensive given the additional requirements for print-quality materials.
- Offline marketing programs tend to cost more.
- Online marketing tools offer a wealth of reporting data that helps you understand how effective your marketing strategies are.
- Because you have access to more granular data more quickly, your targeting for future programs gets better over time with online marketing when you use results from prior programs to improve on your segmentation and offer design.

So what are you waiting for? The reality is that even if you wanted to focus solely on online marketing, your competitors are most likely engaging in some mix of marketing channels to increase visibility overall, so it can seem intimidating to focus on one or the other. However, if you don't have the marketing budget to spend on diversifying your marketing mix like that, know that it's perfectly okay to choose online only. In the end, you will be able to stretch your dollar much further through this channel and to be more methodical about using data to make decisions about what to do next. This can be a tremendously effective channel for converting new business and generating repeat business when done right.

Although you may not start out with an "all online" marketing model, you should be able to "train" your offline customers over time to prefer engaging with your business online by employing the strategies discussed in this chapter.

CREATE AN IN-STORE EXPERIENCE THAT SUPPORTS THE ONLINE MODEL

In Chapter 3, we talked about the importance of a seamless look and feel between your offline business and various online assets, and we discussed how to create promotional campaigns that cross both your offline and online worlds. We also discussed a few tips about how to connect the two experiences on an ongoing basis, such as by posting photos of in-store customers on your social channels. Now, let's look specifically at your in-store experience and develop ways to make going online to engage with your business as attractive as possible.

The most critical part about creating an in-store experience that makes going online attractive is creating a foundation of awareness. If your customers don't know that they can find you online or which channels to use when looking for your business online, then you significantly decrease the chances that your biggest advocates offline will crossover to become your biggest advocates and referrers online. Conversely, if you educate your customers and create awareness about your online presence and don't put forth the necessary time and energy to help these channels come to life, then your audience will quickly dissipate and your effectiveness in those channels will wane over time.

So how much awareness do you need to create for your customers? The short answer is as much as you can manage. Creating awareness and then converting that awareness into action require different levels of effort, and depending on how much time you have to invest in the organic transition between these two customer states, you will want to reassess how much effort you should be allocating to each of your marketing channels. Minimally, you should make sure the following take place as soon as you're committed to investing in certain online homesteads:

- Update your business cards and offline marketing collateral to identify where you spend your time representing your business online. Figure 7.1 shows a fictitious example created on Vistaprint that gives primary real estate to social media presences.
- Another option is to leave the traditional contact information on the front and reserve the entire back side for social addresses with reasons why customers should visit you online, as well as why each social presence is unique from the others (see Figure 7.2).
- Go online and order window decal stickers to place next to your front entrance. To find a Facebook sticker, for example, Google "Facebook Like sticker business" and you'll find a wide variety of window stickers that you can purchase. Figure 7.3 shows a classic "like" sticker that Facebook initially sent to select businesses in 2010.

FIGURE 7.1 Business Card

FIGURE 7.2   Back of Business Card

FIGURE 7.3   Facebook Window Sticker

FIGURE 7.4   Pinterest Window Sticker

Because you theoretically could have a window sticker for each online homestead you focus on, make sure you are consistent with the overall design and sizing for each sticker so you don't clutter your store entrance. You may opt to stay simple with your window sticker (see Figure 7.4) and focus on creating awareness.

- You can also choose to go one step further by incorporating QR code technology to make it easy for customers and passersby to find you online. Customers with smart phones will be able to use one of many free QR code scanning applications to be automatically taken to your selected landing page (see Figure 7.5).
- You can also enable more advanced technologies like near field communication (NFC), which allows users of certain mobile phones to simply swipe their phone over the NFC enabled sticker and be taken to a landing page of your choice (see Figure 7.6). Early technology adopters will appreciate your tech savviness.

Checking these tasks off your list will help you cover minimum ground when it comes to foundational awareness. However, as I noted earlier, there is a difference between awareness and adoption, so it may be a good idea to append your foundational awareness campaign with a few more proactive activities that help drive traffic to your preferred sites:

- **Discuss social media at the point-of-sale.** You can go a step further with framed signage or a stand-up flyer (as discussed in Chapter 3). But the more effective way to increase conversion is to train your staff

FIGURE 7.5   Foursquare Window Sticker with QR Code

FIGURE 7.6   Facebook NFC-Enabled Sticker

to ask buyers during checkout to check-in on your preferred social network. Checkout is the best time for customers to convert during the in-store experience—they've just secured a great find or have just received a fantastic service and are generally feeling the most positive about their experience with your business. Take advantage of that positivity and get them to connect with you online. Try something like this: "Did you know that if you check-in on our Facebook page and show us before you check out you'll automatically get another 10 percent off?" We'll talk about strategies to get your employees excited about going the extra mile here later in this chapter.

- **Get customers' email addresses.** A customer who buys from you but from whom you fail to acquire an email address has a high potential of never returning. Obtaining the email address guarantees that you'll be able to communicate with them over time and keep your business at the top of their minds when it's time to buy again. Make it as easy and attractive as possible for customers to provide their email address to you by incorporating the data collection piece into the purchase experience. For instance, don't just ask if the customer wants to sign up to receive emails from your business. Instead, provide an easily digestible benefit and say, "I'd love to send you coupons once a month so I can give you a discount next time you come in. What's your email address?" or "We host these great free events throughout the year. Do you want me to add you to the invite list?" You won't always need to, but another option is to provide a coupon for their next visit when they sign up for your newsletter.

Institutionalizing these two activities and making them standard practice will significantly accelerate the rate of conversion to an online-first model. Getting a check-in or "like" on the spot guarantees that you'll be able to passively engage with the customer through social channels, actively build relationships online, and convert recurring business over time. Securing the email address gives you the ability to send communications to the customer and drive more revenue-impacting volume over time. Both are critical pieces to your online strategy.

TIP—Convert to Online by Selling the Benefit

With so much unsolicited email being pushed to customers' inboxes, it's no wonder people are more hesitant than ever to share their email addresses with businesses. Especially with online communications, customers want to understand the benefit of sharing this type of personal information with you. If you can very simply explain what you will be doing with this information and why it's a benefit to the customer, you significantly increase your chances of convincing that customer to engage with you online. Here are a few benefits statements that you may consider using:

- Receive special invitations to private events hosted by our business and the local community.
- Keep in touch and receive our monthly/quarterly sales and special offers.
- Receive our monthly newsletter to get great tips and tricks on. . . .
- Join our online community at [site] and get reminders for special events and the things you care about.
- Like our Facebook page to get the best last minute offers and appointment openings.

If yours is an appointment-based business, it's much easier for you to obtain customer email addresses upfront because the stated benefit is clear to the customer. You may simply ask, "Would you like an email reminder or text message for your upcoming appointment?" or "What's your email address and/or cell phone number? I'll make sure you are reminded about your appointment and notified when we have events." Typically the answer will be yes since there is an added convenience factor built in with the reminder.

REWARD CUSTOMERS FOR GOING ONLINE

If you've already implemented foundational awareness around your social connectedness and have integrated data collection into your purchase experience, you can go a step further by leveraging your rewards program and giving more to those who do what you want them to do. We go into more detail about designing effective rewards programs in Chapter 9, but let's talk about some basics here.

With this kind of program, the most important thing is to understand what motivates your customers. Data collection here is important and always beneficial, but you may also already know the answers to some of these questions:

- **What behaviors are you trying to drive?** Identify the specific behaviors in which you want your customers to engage. With a key objective being that you want to convert offline customers to online, consider prioritizing certain online behaviors over offline behaviors. Are you looking to see an increase in social sharing throughout your customers' networks? Do you want to see revenue results in new customer referrals through an online channel? Is the most important thing that your customers are helping drive your online reputation in the form of glowing reviews on specific networks? Select a few of the key behaviors you're looking to influence and use these behaviors as the baseline for your rewards program.
- **What kinds of rewards are you willing to use as leverage?** Consider a mix of discounts, extras, status, and public appreciation. Try keeping things simple in the beginning and creating a straightforward two- or three-tier program that clearly ties the reward to the specific behavior you're targeting. As a side note, you'll be surprised at how ineffective monetary incentives can be at driving motivation, so don't feel like you have to increase discount amounts as a form of increasing your rewards.
- **What gets your customers excited to participate and do more?** More likely than not, you already know a small percentage of loyal customers very well. You may also be engaging with them through

your preferred online channels already. Take what you learn from this segment of your customer base and create opportunities to build stronger relationships with other customers who behave in the same way.

When building a program that drives customer behavior around going online, remember that you probably already have a strong base of knowledge with which to start. You should already have an idea as to how your best customers act and react toward engaging with your business through the various channels you use to deliver communications, and you may already have a good sense of the kinds of incentives, rewards, and accolades that get your best customers excited to participate. Start with what you know and use these tools to design something simple to drive behavior specifically toward online channels.

INCENTIVIZE YOUR EMPLOYEES TO SUPPORT YOUR GOALS

You won't personally be involved in every customer conversation and driving every conversion to online channels, so training your team well and empowering them for success here is critical. If your employees don't support you in converting offline customers to online channels and don't encourage them to engage with your business online, then it'll be difficult for you to succeed here.

Consider building an internal rewards system or contest that incentivizes your team members for going the extra mile and helping drive awareness to your various online social channels. The goals can be team-based and include rewards like monetary bonuses, group outings, or after-hours celebrations. One of our customers, a dentist, had implemented a tiered bonus structure that focused on providing incentives for high satisfaction survey scores and for obtaining a certain number of email addresses as a team. At the end of each month, the dentist would review the team's results in a group meeting so the business as a whole could celebrate its successes together. He also made a point to publically thank the highest individual performers even though the effort was based on team results. This kind of practice creates an environment in which every person on staff is focused on achieving the same goals at the same time, which can be very powerful for your business.

You can also opt to design friendly competitions throughout the year that reward individual behavior. This is an opportunity for you to get creative with the type of behavior you want to reward. For example, what if you were to give bonuses to those who can build the strongest social following on the business Facebook page or who are tagged the most by clients in a given month? Or, how about giving away popular concert tickets to the staff member that gets the most customers to "like" your Facebook page while they are in the store? Make your contests fun and camaraderie building to encourage long-term participation and keep your staff engaged and involved.

Keep in mind that throughout all of this, you'll want to make sure that you're encouraging your team to drive offline to online conversion in a manner that's appropriate for the audience and doesn't feel too pushy. You're not going to have a 100 percent conversion rate, so make sure you're setting realistic goals for your team. Start with a lower target to gain participation and increase excitement levels, then increase those targets as you have more historical data to go by. This will also substantiate the conversation with your team as you start to make your targets more aggressive over time.

Getting customers online is important for many reasons: It's one of the most cost-effective channels for engaging with existing customers, you can easily scale your conversations and create a very personal experience through social outlets, and you can keep your business in your customers' minds through channels on which they are spending their time. Remember, when customers are physically at your business, give them every reason to want to connect with you online so you have the best chance of encouraging return business. It's less about bribery with an incentive and more about delivering on a key benefit that's meaningful to that customer. Some may be immediately interested in the community aspect, and others may only be interested in getting better deals or being reminded about their upcoming appointments. Whatever the reason, whenever you successfully convert a customer from offline to online, it significantly increases your chances of seeing them back at your business again.

CHAPTER 8

Leverage the Magic of Word of Mouth Effectively: Social and Community

We've sprinkled in conversations throughout this book about the importance of leveraging social channels to help build your online presence. We've discussed how to build an integrated marketing plan that takes into account all channels including social media, and we have provided tips on how to continually drive engagement using social media long after the initial sale. In this chapter, we dig a little deeper into the somewhat offline and more traditional notion of "word-of-mouth marketing" and discuss how you can leverage the technology available to you to drive online engagement in similar and measurable ways.

WHY IS WORD OF MOUTH SO POWERFUL?

What's the first thing you do when you're looking for a great place to eat? Most likely, you ask someone you trust for recommendations. If you're in a new town on vacation, you might ask the concierge or desk clerk at the hotel where you're staying. If you're in your hometown, you'll probably ask a friend or relative that you believe has excellent taste or has steered you in the right direction in the past. These habits generally go unchanged when consumers migrate to online channels; most people have taken their offline trusted networks and used them largely as a starting point for building their social circles online. The difference is that when consumers are asking for advice or recommendations online, the questions get published to their entire network at the same time, resulting in feedback that is more diverse and given significantly faster.

Leveraging word of mouth through online and social channels presents a fairly significant upgrade to the offline model for consumers. But consumers aren't the only ones who benefit from increased reach. Corporations have figured out that plugging into the social word-of-mouth cycle and getting involved in the conversation gives them tremendous opportunities to both influence purchase decisions now and in the future. And it's no different for small businesses. You are effectively leveraging word of mouth with the intent to convert customers who are looking to buy now, but more important, you're investing in becoming their preferred future purchase destination.

WORD OF MOUTH FOR THE "NOW SALE"

Like most business owners, you probably recognize how effective leveraging social networks online can be for brand recognition and for influencing the purchase decision over time. Like most businesses, you're probably also very interested in knowing what tricks will influence purchase decisions that generate revenue for your business *now* (as opposed to at an unknown and potentially nonexistent future date). The reality is that while you can certainly increase your level of influence over purchase timing, you will need to be comfortable with increasing the likelihood of certain consequences, such as greater expectations around deep discounts and lower margins, communication burnout, and an increase in opt-outs over time. That said, you absolutely can leverage word of mouth to influence purchase timing—specifically by using the deal structures explained below.

The "You and a Friend" Deal

This is a great approach for businesses for two reasons. First, it turns an existing customer into a returning customer. Second, it encourages that existing customer to bring someone completely new to the business. We've all heard the adage "the best customers are referrals," and it's true. The great thing about this type of customer is that you already know that your existing customer is reliable, and he or she is operating in a socially savvy space. Because the customer is a return visitor, you know that he or she already enjoys being a patron of your business and appreciates what you have to offer. By posting these kinds of deals, you increase your chances of getting more customers like the ones you already have.

Bring-a-friend deals also benefit businesses because they give a very clear indication of how effective your existing customer base can be at driving new patronage on your behalf. Every once in a while—perhaps once a quarter—it's a good idea to offer a such a deal and test word-of-mouth willingness and conversion within your currently active customer base. Of course, in order to leverage the bring-a-friend deal to influence the "now" sale, the deal must offer a higher discount when purchases or appointments are made at the same time. The customer is able to take advantage of a group discount or a better incentive, and the business is able to measure how effective word-of-mouth is in attracting new clients in this manner.

Some factors related to deal design can impact the type of customer you attract. As we've discussed previously, a heavily discounted deal increases your chances of attracting deal-only buyers. You may have to do a little testing in the beginning, but it should be fairly easy after one or two deals to develop an understanding of how to balance the conversion rate from your bring-a-friend deal with the level of discount. It may make sense to start out with some undefined middle ground, perhaps 25 to 40 percent off the retail rate. From there, you can adjust up or down depending on how quickly you are able to achieve your revenue targets. Here are a few bring-a-friend deals you can use as starting points for your testing:

- Buy one item, your friend gets one item half off.
- $25 for you and $25 for a friend when you book a service together.

Don't be afraid to get creative. If your goal is ultimately to get more people in the door—more of the customers like the ones you already have—then incentivize your existing customers to tell your story for you and get those people coming back.

The "Pyramid" Word-of-Mouth Deal

Many people have encountered those pyramid schemes where high school teenagers go door-to-door trying to sell knives. Eventually, those teenagers build an army of other teenagers to sell knives on their behalf, which allows the people at the top of the pyramid to benefit most. You won't be taking advantage of high school students with this deal, but you will be leveraging the same idea here. In this case, your customers are at the top of their own pyramids and you are incentivizing them with deep discounts on the products and services they already buy when they bring new people to your business.

A really easy way of implementing this type of word-of-mouth plan is letting customers know that "for every x number of friends who buy the same product or suite of services (with a referral or other incentive) within 30 days, your next purchase is on us." The key to driving the "now" factor and increasing the speed to purchase is making sure that customers redeem this offer within a specific period of time, hence the 30-day window. As long as you have some way of tracking this—whether it be manually, through your management system, in your QuickBooks software, or simply by trusting customers and enforcing self-reporting—then there's no reason why you can't launch a program like this overnight.

If you have a more sophisticated program in mind, then you want to do your due diligence by running the numbers and ensuring that your business can sustain a level of discounting that you may potentially encounter. Otherwise, it's fine to simply test to see how your customers respond to this type of incentive. But remember, in addition to generating revenue, you're trying to understand how willing your customers are to leverage word of mouth for your business in a way that you somehow can measure. In your testing, you might discover that a simpler approach is better for driving adoption.

The "Make It a Party" Deal

There are obvious benefits to the "make it a party" deal. Instead of your existing customer booking or buying alone, you can extend an offer to a much larger group of new clients at the same time. As it is with the "bring a friend" deal, many of these people are likely to have similar buying habits as existing customers. In order to take advantage of this kind of word-of-mouth deal, you need to have the type of business model that can simultaneously serve a group of customers in the same place. Many service delivery businesses, such as salons, spas, auto detailers, pet caregivers, makeup artists, bowling alleys, or other businesses that can accommodate groups, can easily leverage this offer to scale their visibility.

The other great thing about the "make it a party" deal is that word of mouth takes place up front and is very overt at the time of booking. In addition, it's very easy to track word-of-mouth effectiveness because all customers redeem their services at the same time. Here are a few examples of offers you can try for your business:

- 15 percent off for your entire party
- More is better—an extra 5 percent off for every friend you bring (up to 35 percent off your total bill)
- 10 percent off your party today, and everyone gets 25 percent off their next event here

Again, depending on the level of discounting you're willing to sustain to bring in new clients, you have the opportunity to get as creative as you want. Depending on your objectives, it might make sense for you to launch this kind of word-of-mouth program with a fairly straightforward original framework, and tweak it as you see fit.

There are a variety of flavors when it comes to building programs that nudge your customers along the path of effective word of mouth. Again, it all depends on your ultimate goals, revenue targets, and your ability to execute on these types of deals. You might find that one path makes more sense than another. As a best practice, start with something simple and then build on your word-of-mouth program over time so as not to let complexity keep customers from redeeming deals.

CREATE BUZZ ONLINE WITH CHECK-INS, SHARES, AND MEDIA

If you don't have a time requirement attached to your word-of-mouth program, another effective approach is to encourage employees and customers alike to engage with each other via social media to keep the buzz going online. While you can very effectively tie in the notion of time restrictions through social media, it also might make sense for your business to keep the chatter going through your online channels in general for long-term return.

Promote Checking-In to Drive Buzz

A very easy way to create online buzz—and in turn, potential for word-of-mouth referral—is to encourage your customers to "check in" every time they visit your business. And while you *can* leverage online incentives to promote these check-ins, you may not have to.

Online directories like Yelp and Foursquare have built-in offer programs that allow you to support the check-in habit much more systematically. These programs allow customers to activate certain deals they only get if they take that action. For example, an Indian restaurant on the San Francisco Peninsula called Dosa Republic has an easy check-in offer of 50 percent off Samosa Bits that customers can redeem right after checking in. If you've never checked into this business before, you may not know that the offer exists. But it's a great way for the business to thank regular social media users for letting other people know that they're spending money at this restaurant. Figure 8.1 shows what the offer looks like once you check in on your mobile device through Yelp.

If you want, you can easily increase awareness around the check-in offer by posting signage in an area your customers will see prior to making a purchase. This is yet another easy way to connect the offline and online experiences. If you do post signage, list all of the social networks and online directories on which you have made these types of offers available. Another option is to use your storefront window to exhibit which social networks you've chosen to focus on. This gives you the maximum opportunity available for check-ins and lets your customers know that you're giving them options based on *their* social preferences.

You can take this approach one step further by encouraging customers to share their check-in with their social community. The act of checking in *itself* may not necessarily be social, since the customer doesn't always share their activity with their social networks. Therefore, you may want to encourage them to share their check-ins in exchange for a little something from your business. If you do go this route, make sure that your signage communicates that "something extra" (whatever it is) will be a part of the customer's service experience when he or she checks in. A service-based business might include upgrades as a part of the check-in share. For example, I recently checked in at a local spa online and received an upgrade of aromatherapy oils to the massage service as a thank you for sharing that check-in with my social networks online.

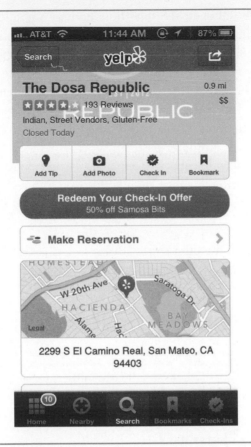

FIGURE 8.1 Yelp Page

This is an easy and inexpensive way for businesses to encourage active checking in and to connect with their customers on yet another platform.

Encourage the "Share"

Before we go any further, let's first clarify what *sharing* means in the context of checking in. Sharing takes place when a consumer posts something about and "tags" your business on his or her own social profile, or when he or she shares something directly from your business Facebook page on his or her own profile. You may or may not need to provide an incentive to encourage your customer base to share—you may find they're already sharing their activity organically. Posts and discussions about things like great purchases or finds, amazing products that your business happens to sell, or even just really great experiences through review syndication and online review sites (like Demandforce) might already be circulating throughout your customers' networks. If this is the case and you're simply not jumping in on the conversation, then you're off to a much better start when it comes to encouraging the "share" within your customer base.

Social sites like Facebook have made it very easy for businesses to encourage sharing amongst their followers. Figure 8.2, for example, shows a shared Facebook post to support the East Bay SPCA.

FIGURE 8.2   Facebook Post Supporting a Local Organization and Event

Businesses benefit from this kind of sharing because social sites provide a nice level of reporting and insight into which types of posts are more popular amongst users, and which they share more than others. Gathering this information allows businesses to better understand what kind of subject matter resonates most with social followers, compels them to take action in the form of sharing, and gives you the information you need to nurture the conversation further and continue to encourage this sharing. For instance, we at Demandforce find the most shareable content has little to do with specific deals, offers, or contests. Rather, light and more fun content like that shown in Figure 8.3 is something that our followers continue to share long after the first three hours of posting.

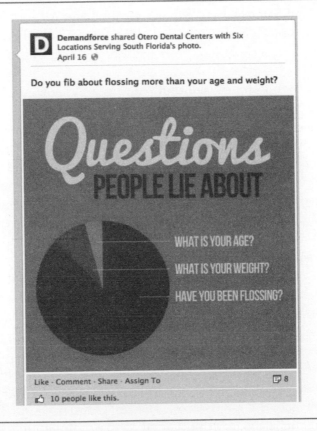

FIGURE 8.3   Fun Facebook Page Content

Consider the ultimate purpose when you are posting highly shareable content that isn't specific to any deal in particular. It should be centered on building brand awareness and recognition as opposed to creating a more immediate purchase conversion. It'll be important over the course of several months to balance these two types of shareable content and provide your social followers with enough variety to stay interested and engaged. Here are some tips on how to create non-deal-specific shareable content for your social sites:

- **Use pictures—lots and lots of pictures.** Include photos of products, people, and animals if you can (and if they have anything to do with your business). The visual element of social media is extremely powerful, especially when you tie the imagery to a message that resonates with your customer base. For instance, Demandforce customer Paul Sammataro at Samm's Heating and Air Conditioning in Plano, Texas, finds that injecting some fun with the business's resident mascot, Pebbles, receives consistently high engagement (see Figure 8.4).

- **Share other people's content.** As you well know, you're not the only business out there creating shareable content. So take advantage of this fact and "crowd source," or leverage other people's content by way of sharing your own content. If you can, go a step further by intentionally sharing interesting content that your own followers have created. Actor and author George Takei is a fantastic example of a social media brand whose content is largely curated by followers. With each of the shares, George simply says "from a fan" to give proper attribution (see Figure 8.5).

- **Inject some fun to break up the business monotony.** Although social sites have been used largely by businesses to engage with their customers, the intent seems to have always been to use social media as a revenue conversion tool. However, consumers are using social media a little differently these days. Therefore, businesses need to inject some fun and color into the conversation to keep their followers coming back for more. It is important for businesses large and small to show some personality and have a little fun on their social sites (refer back to Figure 8.3, for example). This serves two purposes. First, your followers build the habit of sharing as you continue to post a range of content types. Second, they visit your social profile more and more

FIGURE 8.4   Facebook Post Featuring Personal Imagery

to find great shareable content, which helps you get your brand more broadly syndicated.

In the end, *you* know your customers best. Take advantage of this knowledge and start posting content that you believe would drive engagement in the offline world just as much as in the online world. Theoretically, the same people who are walking through your storefront doors are also engaging with you through your online channels and being your strongest social advocates.

Deal sharing is yet another approach customers and businesses can take. Several deal sites have embedded sharing capability into their standard functionality to make it as easy as possible for businesses to

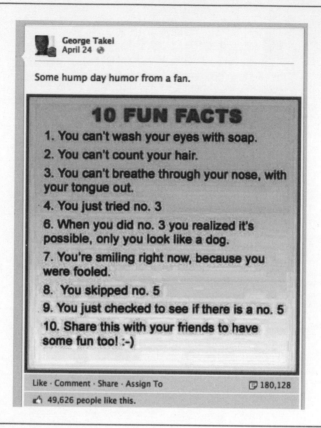

FIGURE 8.5   George Takei Facebook Post

spread the word about the deal and increase total revenue potential. Deal-of-the-day website LivingSocial, for example, has a really great social feature that automatically monetizes word-of-mouth for businesses (see Figure 8.6).

When consumers buy a deal, tell their network that they've done so, and then get three of their friends to buy the same deal, the original purchaser automatically gets the deal for free. While it can be difficult to predict revenue implications for the business itself, combining social sharing and word-of-mouth as effectively as LivingSocial has makes adoption easy for businesses.

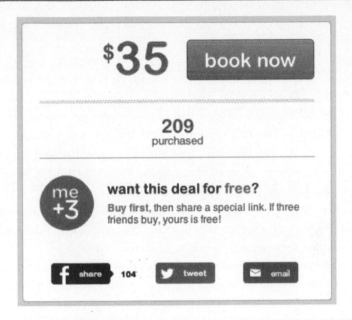

FIGURE 8.6   LivingSocial Promotion

Media Is the Engagement King

In Chapter 2, we discussed ways to bring your business to life on your website by providing a tour of your business, telling your story, or introducing your staff members. In Chapter 5, we talked about the power of customer testimonials when they are put on video. Let's spend a few minutes here talking about the various types of *other* video and media that you can use to increase the buzz about your business online.

If you have access to a mobile device that allows video recording or a camcorder, there's no reason why you can't bring your social sites to life by posting videos to your pages. This is a powerful yet largely underutilized engagement tool for small businesses. Many are under the false impression that they don't have a sufficient background or amount of time to work with these kinds of tools and publish videos. Yet it's much easier to do than most people imagine. Here are some tips to help you get started creating videos primed for social engagement and sharing:

- Keep the videos you create specifically for your social media outlets short and to the point. Try for 60 seconds or less. If your video needs to be longer, keep it under two minutes.
- Focus the content on a single topic as opposed to multiple topics in one video. This provides two benefits. First, you'll be able to extend your video library by spreading out content over time. Second, consumers like to engage with content that comes in the form of a series. This allows you to market your videos as part one, part two, and so on. At Demandforce, any video topic that extends beyond a few minutes in our Whiteboard series at www.youtube.com/DFWhiteboard gets shortened or separated into segments (part 1 and part 2).
- As the narrator of your video, you can't be shy. You need to make sure that viewers will be able to put a face to your voice. So get in front of the camera and introduce yourself before you move on to talking about the topic at hand.
- Try your best to keep the video level. Placing your camera or phone on a stand would be ideal, since it allows you to decrease the motion in your recording. A high level of movement can be very distracting for the viewer. If you don't have a stand for recording, try resting the device on something flat and stable while you record.
- Don't discount the power of a really great video title. Depending on where you post your video, your content may be fully searchable on the Internet, which means that you might eventually start getting organic traffic over time. Make sure your title is both informational and catchy.
- Don't be afraid to ask your viewer to share your videos if that's what your objective is. Have a common and consistent opening and closing for each video that says something like, "Hi this is so-and-so from business name, this video is/was about [subject matter]. If you enjoy watching these videos, please share them so I can keep making them." Your viewers will understand and appreciate that you're asking for them to take a specific action.
- Be aware of lighting. Make sure you *watch* the video before you post anything to the web and verify whether there's enough or perhaps too much or too little light. If it's too difficult to see, your viewer won't

be able to consume the media in the first place. It's worth your time to check and rerecord if necessary versus posting the content to your social site and the web and receiving feedback that the quality was too poor for people to even watch.

- Make sure that the video content is relevant to your business somehow. Of course, that doesn't mean that you can't inject some fun, laughter, color, and a social-media-friendly tone into the video itself. This is an opportunity for you and your business to create a more personal connection with your customers and followers, so take advantage of that.

These are just a few quick tips on how to create fairly simple but engaging videos that people can watch and potentially share on social networks. You may consider creating videos of a higher production quality, and that are perhaps a little longer, on your business website. Your voice might be a little more professional in tone, and your subject matter may be more focused on the business and product or service offering itself. It's perfectly okay to adjust your video's tone and content based on the audience you're trying to reach.

More professional quality videos for websites will probably end up on your social sites and on your online directory profile pages as well, especially if you're syndicating content across your various online assets to maximize visibility. And of course, it's appropriate for your business to be accurately represented in a professional manner wherever you see fit. However, the beauty of social media is that you *do* have the opportunity to be a little bit more personable and fun in nature. We encourage you to leverage social media for all you can and use tools like videos to build relationships and connect with your customers.

CELEBRATE YOUR SOCIALLY CONNECTED CUSTOMERS AND YOUR SOCIAL MEDIA ADVOCATES

You have an unlimited number of opportunities to highlight your socially connected customers within your various marketing channels. Using your social channels to expose your customers to your business and brand can be an extremely powerful way to quickly build stronger relationships with your followers.

Celebrating people via social media does several wonderful things for your brand. You not only get the chance to masterfully incorporate a very *inexpensive* marketing tactic—using real-life examples of buyers to encourage other shoppers to buy—into your overall social strategy, but you're also doing a few other, and perhaps *more important*, things as well. For instance, you are identifying which customers may be willing to be the faces of your social presence (whether they know it or not). These individuals identify themselves as public references for the product or service they purchased, or even just for the business in general. You're also amplifying their inherent excitement levels about having received an excellent service experience, product purchase experience, or overall interaction with your business, and you are giving them a way to remember that experience by sharing it on their social networks. In addition, by celebrating these socially connected advocates, you're slowly building an army of happy customers who are now known entities—people to whom you can reach out who will help spread the word about your business if you ever want to go that route.

You still might not be entirely sure whether the most celebrated or active socially connected customers are your *best*, or even the highest-paying or greatest-revenue customers. But you *do* know that these customers still serve a very important purpose in your overall online marketing strategy. Without a strong base of social advocates, you must rely entirely on your internal team to execute on your social strategy. You don't have that additional amplification from your loyal followers. If a follower comments on a post on your page or social profile, likes something on Facebook, or "+1es" a post on your Google+ page, that information can sometimes get syndicated throughout his or her social network automatically without you ever having to ask for the help. Because of this, you want to make sure that you are supporting this notion of amplification as much as possible. It may be one of the most powerful things that social media can offer for your business in *any* stage of online marketing maturity.

Just as it is with the promotion-based examples discussed earlier in the book, you can highlight your customers and the products or services they've enjoyed for nearly every service your business delivers. Demandforce customer Spodak Dental in Delray Beach, Florida, takes the time to post before and after shots of dental work on their Facebook

FIGURE 8.7   Facebook Post Featuring a Specific Customer

page, but they also like to highlight specific patients like Mary, shown in Figure 8.7.

Formula in Action: Samm's Heating and Air Believes in the Long-Term Power of Social Media

For business owner Paul Sammataro, jumping into social media was not something he thought he had the time to invest in. However with strong encouragement from one of the manufacturers he works

(continued)

(continued)

with, Paul created a Facebook page in 2010. "I went from 2010 and believing in your website being enough of an online presence to now believing that [social media and connection] is what customers and people want. *They want to be able to look at you, see what you're doing, and know who you are,*" says Mr. Sammataro.

Today, he's spending about an hour a day focusing on his social channels and engaging with approximately 1,800 connections weekly. Being able to extend the conversation to hundreds of followers daily has been a worthwhile return on his investment.

Unlike many other small businesses however, Paul strongly believes that social media (as well as other more traditional advertising channels) is a long-term strategy for converting customers. With social channels specifically, he characterizes his time investment as "90 percent relationship building, and 10 percent offer conversion," with his primary focus on Facebook being a more lighthearted conversation, and on Google+ being a platform for a more "ask the expert" and advisory voice.

What works for Samm's Heating and Air? The formula for his business's engagement success story is time tested—the combination of eye-catching and fun images matched up with short descriptions and helpful information grabs readers' attention and drives likes, comments, and shares to increase overall visibility. Paul also recognizes the power of reviews and testimonials as real-life examples throughout social channels and the web that act as persistent reminders as to why prospects and customers alike should buy from Samm's as opposed to any other HVAC provider in the area. His focus on leveraging the Demandforce program to request reviews from customers has garnered feedback from new customers like, "You have a lot of good reviews everywhere I looked."

For small businesses like Samm's Heating and Air, the combination of deciding on a manageable commitment to social media, focusing on the relationship, and leveraging the right tools to get the message across creates an environment in which there is a higher level of credibility built into the business's social and online

(continued)

presences. Customers and browsers alike see the consistent and ongoing engagement, as well as a mix of recent reviews and testimonials that only adds to that credibility. And now when it's time for his online browsers and social lurkers to convert into offline customers, Samm's Heating and Air is well positioned to be the business of choice in his growing network.

Giving those customers willing to be highlighted on your social networks the chance to do so creates a special relationship between the customer and business, so don't be afraid to encourage your customers to interact with your social channels whenever possible. Taking actions like checking in to your business, liking your Facebook page, sharing your current promotions and stories on their social channels, and of course becoming the faces of your business online provide a wealth of benefits for both you *and* them. You will be able to determine pretty quickly what kinds of activities garner the highest interest when it comes to social sharing and participation. And depending on your customer demographic, you may be surprised at how many are openly willing to be a part of your business's story and online community.

CHAPTER 9

Design an Effective Customer Rewards Program

Customer rewards programs are a great way for small businesses to zero in on the behaviors that drive mutual success for both you *and* your most loyal customers. And because the rewards that drive the most activity tend to change over time, don't be afraid to change things up once in a while and test your program benefits. You have to begin, however, by determining what you *want* to happen with this kind of customer interaction.

UNDERSTANDING YOUR GOALS

Before you start designing your rewards program, first consider the outcomes you're trying to drive. Most customer rewards programs typically have one or more of the following goals:

- Drive repeat business.
- Drive new product usage during future visits to broaden the scope of customer spending.
- Drive higher per-visit spending.

If this is the first time you've designed a rewards program, we recommend that you select no more than two goals so that you don't lose focus. Newer businesses are likely looking to encourage repeat business or get existing customers to try new products with each visit. A more mature business with a fairly well-established customer base is probably seeking to build a strong referral system or encourage higher per-visit spending with your existing loyalists. Because our focus is on those who are just getting started in this realm, we'll spend the remainder of this chapter discussing how new businesses can design a rewards program to bring in repeat customers.

IDENTIFYING YOUR REWARD OPTIONS

The first step when identifying your reward is taking a critical look at your sales over the past several weeks. What's selling? What's not? What products or services are customers buying together? For what popular items do you frequently have inventory? Which are easy to keep around? You may also want to ask some of your regular customers some questions, too. What might they consider to be a nice "bonus" to their visit or purchase experience? Put together a short list of potential offerings based on your research and feedback.

The next step is to add items to your short list—just a few high-margin products or services that are easy for you to give away. A classic example of this is a free beverage after every fifth beverage purchase at a coffee shop. If your staff is only you (and perhaps your business partner or spouse), you may also consider trying to pinpoint products or services that have a low material cost but perhaps a higher labor value, such as an esthetician that adds a shoulder massage or a paraffin dip to each facial visit with purchase of a package. Following are a few classic examples by industry that you may consider adding to your short list:

Industry	Possible Rewards
Automotive	Free extended [x]-point inspection, oil change, car wash, interior vacuuming, wiper blades, free local drop-off/pick-up by customer type
Healthcare	Tiered discount co-pay program after [x] visits, a dip in your goodie basket (lip balm, floss, toothbrush, sunscreen, pill box, movie tickets, etc.)
Spa	Product or service upgrade, skin consultation with samples, extended massages or hand/foot massages, wine and/or snacks, access to special parts of the building (Zen rooms, spa pools, deluxe showers, etc.) that would normally be up charged

Industry	Possible Rewards
Hair Care	Free bangs upkeep, deluxe head massage during shampoo, wine and/or snacks, exclusive consultation, product samples
Delivery or moving services	Free furniture padding, upgraded dolly, bucks for future use, preferred time slots
Pet care	Upgraded products during bath, extra time added to walks, pet massages
Cleaning service	Upgraded services such as window blind cleaning, exterior window cleaning, granite sealing, deep carpet cleaning, or extended dusting
Child care	Credits toward aftercare, discounted holiday pricing, tiered pricing for multiples or extended contracts
Food and beverage	Free add-ons, toppings, appetizers, beverages, etc.; access to private dining experiences
Real estate	Upgraded advertising offering, free staging, premium website spots
Financial services	Annual consultations, discounted recommended services, free tax preparation with extended relationship
Printing and publishing	Quantity upgrades, upgrade in paper quality, expedited completion, discounted ancillary services
Consulting	Certain fees waived, upgraded research and recommendation reports, data archiving
Retail	Free or discounted accessories, future bucks with each purchase over a certain dollar amount, gifted services with purchase from a neighboring service-based business

As you can see from the list of possible reward options above, the details of the upgraded offering may be specific to your industry. However, the idea remains the same: You want to extend a special reward to your best customers that may or may not ever be made available to everyone else. Remember, this is an opportunity to make your best customers feel that much more special.

Targeting Rewards toward Socially Connected Customers

Your rewards program is an outstanding way to specifically target your Socially Connected Customers and motivate them to continue their behavior. Instead of designing your rewards around getting customers to spend money with you, consider the benefits of enticing them to take part in other activities that help increase the strength of your online reputation: liking you on Facebook, sharing one of your posts on their own Facebook page, recording video testimonials for your online assets, or writing reviews on one of the online directories you've chosen to manage. Socially Connected Customers are a great way to test the waters on which mix of activities and rewards gets you the biggest bang for your buck.

The options seem endless when you start listing them all out. Your short list may now be a potential top 10 list. That's okay; starting with a high quality list of options allows you to narrow down to the offerings that will ultimately garner the highest interest and most activity from your target segment. Another option to consider is selecting two or three rewards that allow you to broaden your target segment. This method would permit your customers to select their reward at the time of remittance.

UNDERSTANDING TRUE COST

Once you've developed your short list of reward options, you now need to understand the cost associated with delivering each one *en masse*, and factor this cost into the added business's projected revenue. This exercise will likely help trim your 10 or 15 items down to three to five options. It sounds easy enough; however, several unforeseen costs that you need to consider can quickly move an option out of contention.

Let's compare two reward options for a newly opened hair salon that have the same perceived customer value of $25:

Option 1: You are considering offering free blowout and style with high-end products for every $200 service, which carries a retail value of $20. This option has two cost components: labor and raw materials cost. You've estimated the raw materials cost to be about $5 per reward, and the labor cost to be about $15. Easy enough, right? Actually, there is a third cost component—you have to factor in an additional 20 minutes into the appointment to complete the extra work, which costs you an average of $20. In total, each reward costs you $35, which is 75 percent higher in cost than you initially projected, and ultimately discounts the $200 service to $165 for the business.

Option 2: The second option is to gift your salon guests up to $25 worth of hair product from your in-store lines with each $200 visit, and perhaps a travel size product with a $100 visit. This option has a much simpler cost equation: The raw materials likely cost you $13 for every $25 product. Without added "hidden" costs, the reward maintains a flat per-transaction cost of $13. Although the business has a higher raw materials cost in this scenario, the time and labor cost more than make up for it. Your service is only discounted to $187 for a $200 visit.

Option 2 brings the hair salon $22 more per reward redeemed for the same service. It's true that the initial raw materials cost seems more expensive in Option 2. However, you need to account for time and labor costs, as well as the impact it can have on your ability to generate additional revenue from other customers with the time you lose providing extra services. When you consider all the major factors that drive profitability, Option 1's *perceived* value is actually lower than the service's *true* value, making it a less attractive option for the hair salon.

Once you run through cost scenarios for your top 10 list, you'll be able to rank your list by balancing each scenario's true cost and perceived value. From that point, you should be able to select one, two, or three reward options.

Your Program Details

Now that you've done your research on the most attractive rewards, understand true cost associated with giving these products or services away, and have selected the rewards that yield the highest net revenue for your business, it's time to hash out your program details. Here are five key considerations to account for:

1. How frequently do you want to reward your customers? If you're not concerned with frequency as a negative impact to your overall revenue stream, then you may want to consider a program that rewards customers as frequently as you can manage. For instance, with the free beverage after every five purchases rewards program noted earlier, the customer could theoretically receive a reward once a week.

2. How will customers redeem your reward? This is often one of the more challenging questions to answer because you need to identify a process that can be easily carried out within your customer base.

3. How will you keep track of which customers are redeeming the most rewards? (In other words, how do you track your most loyal customers?) This and the next question are often the most difficult to answer because they involve processes that need to be implemented and can be impacted by whatever existing systems you have in place (or a lack of systems). Take the time to try to develop a simple mechanism for keeping track of which customers are redeeming rewards over time so you can benefit in the long term by understanding who your most valuable customers really are.

4. How will you keep track of how many rewards are redeemed overall? If you want to understand which loyal customers are more loyal over time, this is a valuable data point to measure.

5. Do you want to increase the reward value over time to give loyal customers more? Because customer habits change over time and because your more loyal customers may have become acclimated to the types of rewards that your business offers them, it may at some point make sense to increase the value of the reward depending on either how much a customer has spent with you over the years or perhaps how long they've been involved in your rewards program. Depending on the makeup of your customer base, you may want

to select the tiering criteria based on the characteristics of who you believe to be the most loyal to your business.

The quick and dirty way to implement a rewards program is to create an offline wallet card system. This approach puts the onus on the customer to take care of most of the above key considerations (except defining Item 5). Although it's not the most high-tech solution, it gets the job done. Customers also tend to feel more empowered when they always know where they stand with reward attainment. Another variation of this type of system is a card box with customer purchase information that lives at the register or front desk. This method seems to work well with businesses that require a check-in or are session-based, like yoga or dance studios, art schools, and so forth, where it's much less convenient for the customer to carry a wallet card around with them. If you're a Demandforce customer, you can tie rewards directly to referrals and the amount of revenue those referrals have generated for your business directly through your business portal.

If you're looking for a more high-tech solution to designing and managing your rewards system, there are an endless number of providers who would be happy to assist. Depending on the type of rewards program you want to implement, you can leverage companies that crowd source small businesses together to increase the ability for customers to accumulate points more quickly. Belly or LevelUp are two popular options that deliver on consumer rewards in this crowd-sourced manner. Other reward programs like mplifyr (www.mplifyr.com) allow you to create highly customized experiences based on what you know about your customers. Depending on your current needs, you may find going one way versus the other makes more sense for your business right now.

Before you decide on a rewards program provider, be sure to consider your audience prior to jumping on a rewards program bandwagon. You want to make it as easy as possible for your customers to use your program, while also making it easy for you to manage. If your customers do not tend to be early adopters of technology, then it may not make sense for you to invest in a high-tech (and potentially expensive) rewards program right away. Maybe your best strategy is to initially start small and invest in a more high-tech solution when your customers have become acclimated to the notion of a rewards system with your business.

Leverage Rewards to Drive New Customer Acquisition

Regardless of your initial goals in building a rewards program, we always recommend including a bonus for new business referrals and explicitly tying that to your rewards program. This serves two purposes: first, you maintain a single rewards system, which keeps your customers from having to worry about which program they are referring to when redeeming their reward; and second, your customers will connect the referral to a reward over time, which is a great thing because it reinforces the behavior you desire.

The most important thing to keep in mind when rewarding customers for referrals is that you want to reward *both* parties (the referrer and the referee). If you only focus on offering deals for the person referring, the program's adoption rates likely won't be as impressive as they can be, since there is no incentive for the new customers to find their way through your doors. And if you do the opposite—solely rewarding the referee—your existing customers will start to wonder what kinds of "new customer deals" they can get elsewhere. An effective way to balance rewards between the two sides is to implement a "one for you, one for me" strategy. That is, every time an existing customer refers new business, each side gets the same service, product, discount, and so forth. The popular retail daily deal shopping site Gilt.com designed their rewards and referral program entirely around this kind of offer (see Figure 9.1).

For every new purchase made through the share, both you and your friend receive a $25 credit. You don't need a sophisticated management system to keep track of all of the referrals and unique links generated by your customers. Implementing this type of program for a small business can be easy if you have simple processes and rules that your customers can easily follow in order for them to redeem their rewards. For instance, you can put the redemption responsibility entirely on your customers by

Share & Get $25

Join the conversation: Post, tweet and pin the stuff you love.
When your friends join Gilt, you'll get $25 after their first order ships.

FIGURE 9.1   Gilt.com Promotion

instructing them to simply let you know who referred them before they make their purchase so you can look it up (or simply trust them) and apply the credit to their invoice.

Another important guideline to consider is that employees typically represent an underutilized referral pool. Many businesses have some type of referral program for employee referrals; for instance, at Demandforce, we believe the best hires are referrals from existing employees and therefore give bonuses for successfully hired referrals when they join our team. Small businesses can take advantage of this when it comes to both recruiting from a referral pool for new employees as well as when trying to grow the customer base. When you leverage them properly, they can yield multiple benefits for the business, including increased employee satisfaction and retention rates. And the best part is that these rewards don't have to be monetary. Every time one of your employees refers a friend to your business, you can buy them lunch, give them a very public pat on the back, or highlight them on your social channels as an amazing part of your team. There's no need to build a formal structure around rewarding your employees; just make sure you're consistent every single time to drive the positive behavior you're seeking.

Formula in Action: Dave's Ultimate Automotive Gets Loyalty Programs

Dave Erb, owner of Dave's Ultimate Automotive located throughout the greater Austin, Texas, area, has successfully designed a customer loyalty program around driving activity that supports both employee and customer behaviors. "I found that as busy as we were, [managing a complicated loyalty program] was something else that you added onto a service writer's plate. It was too much work and took away from their day," says Dave Erb.

Recognizing the need for simplicity was an important first step in deciding how Dave was going to implement his loyalty program. He decided to forego electronically tying every visit to a customer's loyalty profile and instead had a small plastic keychain tag created that a service writer could easily add to the keychain when customers were getting checked out.

(continued)

(continued)

The second important insight Dave Erb had was that he determined early on what customer behaviors were most important to his business and modeled his loyalty program around those specific behaviors. For Dave's Ultimate Automotive, amount spent, number of visits, and online reputation were the three customer behaviors he felt were most important to driving growth and retention among his customer base. His loyalty program today consists of three levels, which can be attained in any order:

1. Refer five friends and write a review through their Demandforce program.
2. Spend above a certain threshold with the business.
3. Bring your vehicle in a certain number of times.

When each level is attained (Dave uses Demandforce to monitor and verify activity), the service writers simply hole punch the plastic key tag and apply the loyalty reward to the service order. Since the car keys were always something customers would be leaving for service along with the car, the simplistic delivery method made sense. Dave's solution finds an elegant balance between ease of implementation for his employees to promote program adoption and keeping the program and his business's brand in the customers' minds. In addition, because he created specific levels based on actions that would drive his business forward, both his most loyal customers and his business continue to mutually benefit as customers return for each service.

The important thing to note with rewards programs is that your goals and customer base may be different than the business next door; therefore, your rewards program should reflect the unique nature of your business. However, although all businesses are different, the underlying goals still remain very similar: Be specific about what you want to get out of your program so you can design one that will give the results you're looking for.

CHAPTER **10**

"I Brake for Testing": Measuring Success and Tweaking Your Program over Time

In this chapter, we will focus on the basics of testing your online marketing program over the course of your 12-month marketing plan. Testing is a frequently underutilized marketing tool by small business owners because it takes time to test, it's often difficult to know what exactly you should be testing, and it can be difficult to interpret results to make changes to your programs. But even given all that, running some basic testing strategies to validate your marketing plan is extremely important, especially when you're working with a limited marketing budget.

WHY TEST?

Without some level of testing to validate the marketing spending and overall marketing mix, it's difficult as a small business owner to justify increasing your spending over time for more effective programs and taking away from less effective programs that you might be more attached to. Marketers have the tendency to stick to programs they know and that have proven effective in the past. However, the reality we're faced with today is that because the consumer–seller relationship has shifted so dramatically, the old programs may not work quite as well and for as long as they used to.

Testing also gives you the opportunity to validate some assumptions that you've made about your customer base. For instance, if you believe that your customers respond better to the "dollar off" discount as opposed

157

to the "percent off" discount based on general sales numbers, but you don't know where these customers in general are coming from, you may be missing out on an opportunity to maximize conversion from your existing customer base while you could still be taking in that additional revenue from new customers already walking through the door. With your attrited or dormant customer base, testing plays a particularly important role because you're less likely to have a strong understanding of what discount level or promotion type is just right in order to convert this segment back into buyers. That dormant customer base represents the highest potential revenue lift for your business, primarily because those customers represent revenue that you would not have previously booked, so focusing some effort on effectively testing for the right promotions here is a win for your business.

Perhaps the most interesting reason as to why testing is important is that as you continue to evolve your marketing and advertising promotions, content, collateral, and voice, you have the added benefit of keeping your audience engaged and interested in what you have to say. Just like with any other relationship, saying the same thing over and over again with the same look and the same feel can get old pretty quickly, so why would you do that with your customers?

Define Testing Goals before Designing Your Test

Before you start brainstorming the various ways that you're going to test for success, first consider what it is that you're looking to get out of the test in general. In Chapter 3, when identifying the connectors between your offline and online marketing worlds, we first started with understanding the business's goals with this particular promotion. With testing, the starting point is no different. Following are some examples of realistic testing goals based on common business objectives.

Business Objective A	Testing Goals
Increase return rate for dormant or attrited customers	Understand how aggressive the business needs to be with the promotional mix to reconvert this segment

With this business objective, you are recognizing that a "lost" or nonreturning customer may need a more aggressive offer to do business with you again. But, how aggressive do you need to be? Is it worth it for you to break even just to get another chance to deliver an experience that will get them to come back voluntarily? Or, are you willing to take a revenue hit for the same opportunity? These are all considerations you will have to take into account when building your test plan.

A secondary concern to take into account is that there may be a reason that customer attrited in the first place. For instance, they may be "deal only" shoppers that may return only if the deal is discounted deeply enough. Although these types of customers provide a nice revenue and cash flow push when you need it, the overall impact to your bottom line can be extremely detrimental over time. As a business owner, you need to decide whether you want to continue to fuel that customer segment for the long term.

Business Objective B	Testing Goals
Decrease revenue impact of last minute offers	Understand the minimum discount that can be applied to last minute offers while still reaching the target booking

Last minute deals are an incredibly effective tool for making sure your books continue to stay full through any potential rough patches. After all, it's better to have a full book at a discounted rate than to have empty spots, right? However, as I've stated throughout this book, there is a careful balance between leveraging this tool for its intended purpose and training your customer base to wait it out until they receive a better deal. The testing goal in this case should have the business outcome of increasing last minute bookings without seeing a decrease in advanced bookings.

Business Objective C	Testing Goals
Increase effectiveness of email marketing to generate revenue	Understand the types of conversations and incentives that generate the highest engagement and/or conversion through email marketing

You may already be utilizing email marketing to engage with your audience on a regular basis. But, do you know how effective these tools are when it comes to engagement and ultimately conversion into paying offline customers? The beauty of having a business objective involving effective utilization of an online tool is that oftentimes you'll have access to significantly more data to make decisions than if you were testing offline methods.

Effective testing with online marketing tools frequently involves A/B testing, or measuring the difference between one variation and a control to random customer segments. In order to leverage this kind of testing methodology, however, you want to first hypothesize what may happen and build a target outcome to measure effectiveness. For instance, if you're testing two offers in an email, one that is 15 percent off and one that is 25 percent off, my hypothesis may be that the two discounts will generate the same number of offline conversions and foot traffic in the end (or, that the higher discount does not generate a higher return or more revenue). You may find, however, that even though the same number of customers converted through each discount type, the overall revenue per customer was higher with the higher discount rate (or, the higher discount does in fact generate a higher average return per customer). Running these kinds of tests periodically will ensure that you're making smart decisions about what your next promotion will be and that you're maximizing each marketing channel as much as possible.

From the examples above, you can see that testing plays a critical role in both ensuring that your business converts as many of those online conversations to offline sales as possible and helping you maximize revenue potential with any given piece of the overall marketing program. For the remainder of this chapter, we'll refer back to these three business objectives to introduce easy-to-implement testing plans that won't require a marketing degree to execute.

TESTING MADE EASY

When it comes to the ins and outs of testing, stick with the concept that "simple is better." Having too many variables in a single test will cloud the results, as well as your ability to identify which variable (or combination of variables) truly impacted the outcome. In addition, more complicated testing plans can take much longer to deliver data that you can use to make decisions. For our purposes, we'll focus on these four easy testing strategies that won't break your bank or require too much of your team's time to execute and interpret results:

1. Single channel testing
2. Symptoms as an early indicator of outcomes
3. Small segment testing
4. Promo and referral codes

Single Channel Testing

Single channel testing is a low-cost way to understand effectiveness prior to investing your marketing allocation toward a full-blown cross channel marketing program. Typically businesses will test via email marketing as the lowest cost channel, but you can just as easily run tests through your social channels or even focus on small segments through offline channels to keep costs down if you really wanted to.

The objective of single channel testing is to be able to quickly test your hypothesis, get results fast, adjust as you need to, and test again if necessary. To test outcomes for Business Objective A (increasing return rate for dormant or attrited customers), you might consider leveraging email marketing since you can easily segment your offer based on any number of variables. Demandforce customers may segment by offering a higher last minute discount to those you know haven't been in for longer than 12 months but never wrote a review for you, and then offer a slightly less aggressive offer to those who haven't visited in more than 12 months but at some point provided a review on your business. If you're not a Demandforce customer but have access to similar data within your management system, you can easily export and create segmentations in Excel for uploading to your email marketing tool. The hypothesis to test in this scenario would be whether the interest conversion, or number of in-bound inquiries your business receives, is greater with one offer over another.

Business Objective C (maximizing the effectiveness of the email marketing program) is an excellent example of single channel testing where the outcomes may not necessarily impact your other marketing channels. Usually, however, when you opt to test in a single channel, you're testing a smaller segment with the intent of proving or disproving a hypothesis and then potentially rolling it out across your other crosschannel efforts.

The other great thing about single channel testing, especially through online marketing channels, is that you can usually get results within a week or two of launching your test. This makes for quick turnaround to make a decision and, in turn, a quick full-program roll out.

Symptoms as Early Indicators of Outcomes

If you've already done some testing in the past or you feel like you have a pretty good understanding of how the various segments within your customer base react to the marketing programs you've historically run, you can use this testing method to quickly revalidate prior assumptions you've already validated or to quickly test something new and look for common symptoms (or patterns that you recognize that were early indicators of program outcomes) to correlate against.

Let's use Business Objective B (decreasing the revenue impact of last minute offers) as the case study for this test. Assuming that you've already found that $30 off a $100 service (Deal 1) is the ideal price point to quickly book those same day last spots in your book when you happen to have them, you now need to figure out what the right discount is for a $65 service (Deal 2). Typically with Deal 1, all of the spots are filled within one hour of posting through social networks. For Deal 2, you first try to post an offer for $50 for the $65 service, which has some takers, but not all spots are filled. In your next test, you instead try $45 for the $65 service, which gets all of the spots filled in a similar manner as Deal 1's behavior. Because you're testing for the balance of maximum revenue against minimum open spaces, it's important that the business is able to fill up the same day or next day spots, so the symptom you're trying to model after is how long it takes to fill the same number of spots.

When testing for symptoms or customer behaviors, always start off with more conservative offers and work your way down. In the case of Deal 2, the $20 discount represents a larger percentage discount than Deal 1, so the overall revenue impact is higher. However, you were still able to effectively minimize the overall revenue impact by applying the smallest discount necessary to achieve the same effect as Deal 1, which was to book all of the open slots within one hour.

Small Segment Testing

Small segment testing is a great way to get valuable feedback on what works without running lengthy campaigns or delivering resources to fulfill services you've overcommitted. You also have the added benefit of hedging against losses if you find that the test yields poor results or, on the flip side, you were far too aggressive with your discounting and generate negative revenue.

The easiest way to launch a small segment test is to either limit the number of redemptions that can be turned in per promotion, limit the number of customers you make your offer to, or create a promotion that uses some combination of the two. When used as a way to limit the sample size, marketers typically want to understand the potential change in interest levels across a set of promotion ranges, customer demographic, or some other segmentation more than anything else. For instance, if the business has multiple locations throughout a greater metropolitan area, they may want to test how effective a promotion is with each of those areas independently over a short time period and then compare results. The business may find that there are unique characteristics of each customer demographic at each location that warrants more customized promotions per location. They may also find over the course of their small segment testing efforts that there are no significant differences between the locations and decide to roll out brand-wide marketing campaigns with confidence.

Here are a few ways to leverage small segment testing to more easily gain insight into how successfully your campaign might perform with a larger audience:

- **Limiting redemption period:** Limiting the redemption period can be very beneficial for small businesses both as a tool to drive a surge in traffic, as we discussed earlier when it comes to creating a sense of urgency with promotions, and as a protective measure to hedge against when you're testing new promotions.
- **Limiting redemption volume:** This is a great tool to use both when you actually have a limited volume of product or service to bring to market and when you want to test for adoption at a certain discounted rate.
- **Segmenting demographic:** A very common way to limit the sample size is to segment your customer base by very specific characteristics.

Segmenting by demographic can be very beneficial in your testing plan when you are using a subset of a larger segmentation that you're trying to test for (e.g., a 50-person random sample of 18- to 21-year-old mobile users out of a larger segmentation of 1,000). Keep in mind, however, that by using demographics to segment, you are introducing a variable to your testing plan that needs to be accounted for when reviewing results. For instance, if you segment for 18- to 21-year-old mobile users, it's very possible that your test results may differ than if you segmented for 45- to 55-year-old multiple car owners.

Just like with the earlier testing methods, small segment testing delivers quick results while protecting your bottom line, and without bombarding your entire customer base with heavy promotions. With this testing method, however, be aware that the results may not always be indicative of how your general customer base will behave.

Measuring at the Point of Sale—Promo and Referral Codes

If you have the ability to do so, implementing a system that allows you to track marketing efforts and purchases with a coding methodology can be extremely beneficial. Even if you don't have a way to track the marketing piece, being able to tie code redemption at the point-of-sale can be an extremely valuable and fairly easy way to test and measure program effectiveness. If you're using a management system in your front office or at the register, you should be able to enter a certain number of promotion codes as the baseline for what you want to measure. For the sake of simplicity and to make it easy for your employees to adopt, select only a few things to measure. Here are a few to consider tracking at the point-of-sale:

- **How frequently are referrals coming in, and who is doing the referring?** Small businesses depend on word-of-mouth and referrals as key drivers for new business, so you should be tracking as best you can where your referrals are coming from. Knowing which referral codes are being redeemed and with what frequency can be a powerful indicator of where you should focus your efforts in this area. As a Demandforce customer, we will automatically tell you which of your customers are your best referral champions if they are doing so through the communications we send on your behalf.

- **How successful is the campaign into which you're investing the most offline marketing dollars?** If you have a difficult time tracking the return on investment (ROI) because you don't have an easy way to report on results, recording redemption at the point-of-sale may be the easiest and most accurate way of reporting on ROI. You may find that 30 to 60 days after investing a large percentage of your marketing budget into an offline channel you see no significant increase in offer redemption—both in general and through the specified promo codes—which could be an indicator that either your promotion was not on target for the chosen segment, or that the promotion was not on target for the chosen delivery channel. Either way, if you don't track for redemption here, then you will never truly know.

- **How successful are certain low-margin products or services and the promotions you publish for them?** This is important to measure over time because it can give you insight into how you might want to change your product and service offerings. If you are taking the time to train staff on delivering a low-margin product or service and then over time still need to further discount in order to consistently convert purchases, it might be worth replacing that product or service with an offering that will both provide higher revenue per visit and higher volume.

Remember, when it comes to testing, first take the time to understand what your business objectives are and then shape your testing goals to be able to answer any outstanding questions you may have. Testing doesn't have to be complicated; in fact, the more simplistic you can make your testing plan and the fewer variables you introduce, the cleaner your results will be and the easier it will be for you to make decisions based on the testing outcomes.

Summary

Getting started with building and then executing an online marketing plan can seem like a daunting task for anyone who has never done this before. As a small business owner, the stakes may seem exponentially higher because you're building a plan for a business that is often rooted in something you're deeply passionate about or you have some personal financial responsibility tied to the business's success.

The good and bad news is that you're not alone. On the one hand, with well over 27 million small businesses in the United States[1] alone, as reported by the U.S. Small Business Administration, small business owners are continuing to fuel employment and drive the U.S. economy. This means that as a new business owner, you have a lot of support and can harness the shared experiences and best practices of other small business owners to get off to the right start. On the other hand, with only 45 percent of small businesses established in 2004 still open in 2009,[2] competition to stand out and gain market share needs to be an ongoing primary focus for small business owners.

In order to get ahead and stay ahead, small business owners need to be thoughtful about where and how they are spending both their time and their marketing dollars so they can maximize their overall return. It's an easy formula that you can follow whether you have any marketing experience or not:

- Create a foundation for your online reputation that you can build on and build a reasonable online marketing plan for your business that you can stick to.
- Leverage technologies that enable you to deliver exceptional experiences, connect with your customers and prospects where they are, and provide customers with modern-day conveniences they expect.
- Enable, empower, and reward your tech-savvy customers and social advocates to be your most effective marketing channel.

---

[1] www.fas.org/sgp/crs/misc/R41520.pdf.
[2] www.cnn.com/2012/07/13/politics/small-business-btn.

- Test your marketing plan and measure for results so you can keep refining your marketing plan over time.

Remember, take things one step at a time and don't be afraid to get started small today—your online marketing plan and online reputation build on themselves year after year, so the sooner you get started, the sooner you'll be on the right track to converting online conversations to offline customers.

WORDS OF WISDOM FROM DEMANDFORCE CUSTOMERS

As I was writing this book, I had the great pleasure of interviewing a number of Demandforce customers to hear their stories and learn about how their unique businesses were built from the ground up, how they evolved over time, and how they are managed today. The most interesting outcome of these interviews may not be anything new to you as a small business owner, but it certainly reinforces my deep respect and gratitude for people taking the plunge into running a small business.

Their formula for success is like grandma's chicken soup recipe— there's a secret ingredient in every single recipe that may sound similar on the surface, but is really a little bit different from one grandmother to the next. A pinch of salt to one person is really a pinch and a half to another. And in the world of small business, one person's "best practice" may not work as well for another due to an infinite number of variables. Simply said, there is just no *one* way to get it right.

Although this book takes you through the most common best practices as they relate to online marketing and how small businesses can get a jump start, there are also a number of other key messages that I collected from these interviews, and I'm honored to be able to share a few of these "words of wisdom" from just some of our favorite customers.

The Secret Sauce

As I was interviewing Dr. Craig Spodak of Spodak Dentistry in Delray Beach, Florida, I was impressed with a number of philosophies he employed in his business practice. We went into great detail on Dr. Spodak's marketing plan, referral programs, and ongoing promotions. Throughout the interview I continued to be drawn in by the doctor's sheer willingness to be an early adopter with new marketing trends and also to test methodically for results.

There was one thing that really stood out to me: Dr. Spodak consistently referred back to the importance of quality execution no matter what part of the business we were talking about:

> I think the secret sauce is the execution of what you're promoting. Everyone looking outside in looks at the promotion itself that makes it a success. In reality, it's how the product or service is executed at the business that creates the success.

> Execution is fundamental. You have to have a values-based business that your employees are engaged in. Your team has to feel like they are a part of [the business's success]. If you can do this, no matter what, the promotion will be executed in the right way.

Even if you're not ready to invest a large percentage of what marketing budget you may have into online marketing, making sure that every single customer interaction is the absolute best it can be is absolutely critical and perhaps the most important "secret sauce" to any promotion, campaign, or just a regular day on the job:

> Taking exceptionally good care of one person is equal to $100,000 of advertising. Everyone is talking about "How do I get 20 new patients this month?" But just take care of the two patients you do get and let them do the talking for you.

> If we get one bad review, no matter what it is, we're on it. We'll make it right. People think it's just about advertising. Advertising is a drug that once you start, you never get the same high as the first spend. Then you need to advertise to get more. It's almost better to advertise less and let the people do your advertising for you. That's why Demandforce is good. It allows for the internal control system to show you how well you're taking care of your customers so you can continue to improve your business.

In the end, for Dr. Spodak and for many of our customers, leveraging tools to measure and improve on their business practices is a foundational means for ensuring that they are delivering on what they need and want to so when it comes time to leverage word of mouth, publish promotions for new customer acquisition, and ask for referrals, they can do so with confidence. Most important, having that secret sauce in place enables them to trust that they will be able to both grow revenue as well as consistently add to their online reputation over time.

It's *Your* Business

Dr. Penn Moody of Moody Eyes in Indianapolis, Indiana, is an engaging and vibrant character—and at 62, he's also a lone advocate in his age demographic for the necessity of social media in business as a powerful relationship-building tool. Since getting an early start in 2008 with Facebook and Twitter, Dr. Moody and his team have worked to develop their own unique voice that hones in on the core of why the social media revolution began in the first place:

> We focus on great stories that are personal. We're human. Social media is about humans connecting. Some posts will be informative, but you can give information through story versus just information. We also post a lot of pictures and our followers love engaging with questions.

Dr. Moody takes things a step further by having almost completely deemphasized the usage of promotional campaigns through this channel in his online marketing strategy to date. Although he and his team are considering integrating the social channel into the promotional mix, Dr. Moody still stays true to his core philosophies regarding social media as a relationship-building tool:

> Sure, I'm looking at the idea of posting offers—I think that's a really nice way to use social media if it's not over used. You don't want to put too much self-promotion. Think of it as if we're sitting around dinner and having drinks. Don't sell—it has to be a conversation.

Perhaps even more compelling is Dr. Moody's philosophy—one that he stressed both throughout our conversation and in his daily practice—around the importance of business owners taking ownership of how their business is represented in any marketing channel:

> I think the bottom line for optometrists is the same bottom line for every business no matter how big or how small. In the end, services like Demandforce can be really helpful, but you have to make sure that the message you're telling is the message you want to tell. It's still your message and your business. I see some of my colleagues—they hire a service and they say "you take care of it"—but they need to make sure they're telling your story because they're representing you and it's your business.

The stark reality of Dr. Moody's statement speaks to a challenge that Demandforce has at times as well. Small business owners will often sign up for a marketing program—one that, in our case, enables that business to leverage a variety of online channels to both amplify their message and systematically source consumer review feedback—expecting something much more turnkey, specifically around the message design as well as message amplification. Dr. Moody, however, continues to be a shining example of a small business owner who takes full ownership of his brand and brand message, which does mean spending a bit more in the beginning investing the time or resources to learn how to maximize his tools.

In the end, no one knows your business like you as a small business owner do, and it remains your responsibility to ensure that you understand and learn how to use the tools you choose to leverage for your business to maximize your probability for success.

Use Your Tools to Get the Kinds of Customers You Want

Passionate about building an environmentally friendly business, Dr. Nammy Patel of Green Dentistry in San Francisco, California, initially invested heavily in becoming a LEED Certified Green business and continues to invest in new, safer technologies as they become available to the industry. A long-time customer of Demandforce, Dr. Patel is also a strong advocate for the need for small businesses to leverage technology for added customer convenience before they ever ask for it.

This commitment to making her dream a reality came at a price that any small business owner can understand. Oftentimes, sourcing green or sustainable supplies, products, technologies, and services can be significantly more expensive than their less environmentally friendly counterparts. "When I first opened my practice, I would just have people walking through the door from all walks of life," Dr. Patel said as she described the early days of being a small business owner.

Over the years, Dr. Patel has continued to stay true to her mission. While she has established her practice as a standard of excellence in sustainable business within the San Francisco Bay Area, she has been able to evolve her marketing strategy to attract patients who want exactly what she has to offer:

> Now, I'm able to be more selective. I want to work with people who are more interested in their health as opposed to just when there's a problem. I want to work with people who want to be educated. Today, I run promotions that target a more mature age group, as well as those who are interested in receiving the kinds of services I'm passionate about delivering such as healthy gums and preventative care.

Dr. Patel's combined efforts around overall business branding, search engine optimization and website keywords, and marketing promotions enable her to specifically target potential patients and garner return business from patients whose values are aligned with her own. She's redesigned her website several times over the years to continue to refine her messaging around sustainable and environmentally friendly technologies, ensuring a combination of the right keywords that consistently deliver high search results for her practice. In addition, she has designed a simple yet effective referral program that today helps generate most of the practice's new business through referrals.

Her ability to both tie her passion to a successful business and reposition herself in the marketplace as a niche provider, through a combination of promotional and targeting efforts, is a testament to Dr. Patel's marketing savvy and willingness to keep on improving the business, something for which business professionals are certainly all striving.

Appendix

RECOMMENDED READING

This book is intended to give you a "hit the ground running" introduction to online marketing for small businesses. Things evolve quickly in the world of online marketing, so if you'd like to stay up-to-speed as trends shift, here are some recommended books and blogs to read.

Blogs

Intuit Small Business Blog: blog.intuit.com

Mike Blumenthal's Blog—Understanding Google Places & Local Search: blumenthals.com/blog

Google and Your Business: googleandyourbusiness.blogspot.com

Social Media Examiner: socialmediaexaminer.com

Small Business Search Marketing: smallbusinesssem.com

Small Business Trends: smallbiztrends.com

Books

Creating Customer Evangelists: How Loyal Customers Become a Volunteer Sales Force, Ben McConnell, Jackie Huba (Kaplan Publishing, 2002)

Word of Mouth Marketing: How Smart Companies Get People Talking, Andy Sernovitz (Kaplan Business, 2006)

Guerrilla Marketing: Easy and Inexpensive Strategies for Making Big Profits from Your Small Business, Jay Conrad Levinson (Houghton Mifflin, 2007)

Landing Page Optimization: The Definitive Guide to Testing and Tuning for Conversions, Tim Ash, Maura Ginty, Rich Page (Sybex, 2012)

The Facebook Guide to Small Business Marketing, Ramon Ray (Wiley, 2013)

Acknowledgments

This book is really the collective effort of the incredibly hard working team at Demandforce. Since joining the Demandforce team in 2010, I've found nothing but a deep inherent passion for helping small businesses stand out from the millions of other North American small businesses and find their own unique online voices. Our continued focus on educating customers, not only on how to use Demandforce's many features but also empowering anyone willing to listen about how to become better online marketers, has proven beneficial for thousands of small business owners looking to get ahead and stand out from the pack. Think of this book as an aggregation of everything we try to teach our customers over the life of their relationships with us, all wrapped up in one package.

Special thanks to Demandforce's president and founder, and my mentor, Rick Berry, for supporting me every step of the way through this project, and for always challenging me to incorporate my personal passions into my career. To those of you on the Demandforce team who provided feedback, fact-checking support, downloadable worksheets, and editorial comments—Lauren Denault, Sylvia Chow, Carola Ponce, Cory Tan, Patrick Barry, Becca Piastrelli, and Jennifer Piumarta, in particular—thank you for your continued assistance through this long process. Last but not least, thank you to my husband, Tom, for an infinite number of things, but in this particular instance, for staying up with me late nights and early mornings to make our crazy schedules seem perfectly normal.

Index